W9-CAS-932

Publications International, Ltd.
Favorite Brand Name Recipes at www.fbnr.com

Copyright © 2004 Publications International, Ltd.
All rights reserved. This publication may not be reproduced or quoted in whole or in part by any means whatsoever without written permission from:

Louis Weber, CEO
Publications International, Ltd.
7373 North Cicero Avenue
Lincolnwood, IL 60712

Permission is never granted for commercial purposes.

Favorite Brand Name is a trademark of Publications International, Ltd.

All recipes and photographs that contain specific brand names are copyrighted by those companies and/or associations, unless otherwise specified. All photographs *except* those on pages 55, 95, 101, 185, 223, 275 and 297 copyright © Publications International, Ltd.

Toll House is a registered trademark of Nestlé.

Some of the products listed in this publication may be in limited distribution.

Pictured on the front cover *(clockwise from top right):* Mocha Nog *(page 240),* Buttery Almond Cutouts *(page 310),* Cheese Pine Cones *(page 18)* and Roast Turkey with Pan Gravy *(page 200).*
Pictured on the back cover *(left to right):* Herb-Roasted Racks of Lamb *(page 150),* Golden Apples and Yams *(page 102)* and Cranberry Cheesecake Muffins *(page 82).*

ISBN: 0-7853-8645-9

Library of Congress Control Number: 2003098913

Manufactured in China.

8 7 6 5 4 3 2 1

Microwave Cooking: Microwave ovens vary in wattage. Use the cooking times as guidelines and check for doneness before adding more time.

Preparation/Cooking Times: Preparation times are based on the approximate amount of time required to assemble the recipe before cooking, baking, chilling or serving. These times include preparation steps such as measuring, chopping and mixing. The fact that some preparations and cooking can be done simultaneously is taken into account. Preparation of optional ingredients and serving suggestions is not included.

Contents

Joyous Starters

Spinach Cheese Bundles

1 container (6½ ounces) garlic- and herb-flavored spreadable cheese
½ cup chopped fresh spinach
¼ teaspoon black pepper
1 package (17¼ ounces) frozen puff pastry, thawed
Sweet and sour or favorite dipping sauce (optional)

Preheat oven to 400°F. Combine spreadable cheese, spinach and pepper in small bowl; mix well.

Roll out one sheet puff pastry dough on floured surface into 12-inch square. Cut into 16 (3-inch) squares. Place about 1 teaspoon cheese mixture in center of each square. Brush edges of squares with water. Bring edges together up over filling and twist tightly to seal; fan out corners of puff pastry.

Place bundles 2 inches apart on baking sheet. Bake about 13 minutes or until golden brown. Repeat with remaining sheet of puff pastry and cheese mixture. Serve warm with dipping sauce, if desired.

Makes 32 bundles

Holiday Appetizer Puffs

1 sheet frozen puff pastry, thawed (½ of 17¼-ounce package)
2 tablespoons olive or vegetable oil
Toppings: grated Parmesan cheese, sesame seeds, poppy seeds, dried dill weed, dried basil leaves, paprika, drained capers, pimiento-stuffed green olive slices

Preheat oven to 425°F. Roll pastry on lightly floured surface to 13-inch square. Cut into shapes with holiday cookie cutters (simple-shaped cutters work best). Place on ungreased baking sheets.

Brush cut-outs lightly with oil. Decorate with desired toppings.

Bake 6 to 8 minutes or until golden. Serve warm or at room temperature.

Makes about 1½ dozen appetizers

Bacon & Cheese Dip

2 packages (8 ounces each) reduced-fat cream cheese, softened, cut into cubes
4 cups shredded reduced-fat sharp Cheddar cheese
1 cup fat-free evaporated milk
2 tablespoons mustard
1 tablespoon chopped onion
2 teaspoons Worcestershire sauce
½ teaspoon salt
¼ teaspoon hot pepper sauce
1 pound turkey bacon, cooked and crumbled

Slow Cooker Directions
Place cream cheese, Cheddar cheese, evaporated milk, mustard, onion, Worcestershire sauce, salt and pepper sauce in slow cooker. Cover and cook, stirring occasionally, on LOW 1 hour or until cheese melts. Stir in bacon; adjust seasonings. Serve with crusty bread or fruit and vegetable dippers.

Makes about 1 quart

Stuffed Pesto Torta

2 tablespoons olive oil
1 cup chopped onion
3 cloves garlic, minced
1 can (14½ ounces) Italian-style tomatoes, undrained and chopped
2 tablespoons tomato paste
2 teaspoons dried Italian seasoning
½ teaspoon salt
½ teaspoon red pepper flakes
1 package (3 ounces) cream cheese, softened
½ cup (2 ounces) freshly grated Parmesan cheese
⅓ cup whole-milk ricotta cheese
¼ teaspoon black pepper
1 pound fresh uncooked Italian sausage, casings removed
1 package (17¼ ounces) frozen puff pastry, thawed
½ pound thinly sliced Gruyère or mozzarella cheese
6 tablespoons purchased or homemade pesto
1 egg yolk
1 teaspoon water

Heat oil in medium saucepan over medium-high heat until hot; add onion and garlic. Cook 2 minutes or until onion is tender. Add tomatoes with juice, tomato paste, Italian seasoning, salt and red pepper; bring to a boil. Reduce heat to low; simmer, uncovered, 30 minutes or until mixture reduces to 1⅓ cups. Remove from heat; set aside.

Meanwhile, combine cream, Parmesan and ricotta cheeses and black pepper in medium bowl; beat with electric mixer at medium speed until smooth. Set aside.

Brown sausage in large skillet over medium-high heat until no longer pink, stirring to separate meat. Drain sausage on paper towels; set aside.

Preheat oven to 375°F. Roll out 1 pastry sheet to 13-inch square on lightly floured surface with lightly floured rolling pin. Press pastry onto bottom and up side of 9-inch springform pan. (Pastry will not completely cover side of pan and will hang over edge in places.)

continued on page 10

Stuffed Pesto Torta, continued

Layer 1/2 of cooked sausage on bottom of pastry shell. Top with 1/2 of reserved tomato sauce mixture, spreading evenly. Drop 1/2 of cream cheese mixture by heaping teaspoonfuls over tomato sauce mixture. Arrange 1/2 of Gruyère in pastry shell, forming solid layer. Spread pesto evenly over Gruyère with small metal spatula. Arrange remaining Gruyère over pesto, forming another solid layer. Drop remaining cream cheese mixture by heaping teaspoonfuls over Gruyère. Top with remaining tomato sauce mixture. Layer with remaining cooked sausage. Trim overhanging pastry to an even height with paring knife. Fold pastry over filling.

Roll out remaining pastry sheet to 12-inch square on lightly floured surface; trim to 8-inch circle. Make decorative pastry cut-outs from excess dough, if desired. Beat egg yolk and water in small bowl with fork until blended. Lightly brush beaten egg mixture on pastry around filled torta. Carefully place 8-inch circle of pastry over torta, pressing gently to adhere. Lightly brush top crust with beaten egg mixture and arrange pastry cut-outs on top. Brush cut-outs with beaten egg mixture.

Bake 1 hour or until pastry is golden. Let stand 15 minutes on wire rack. To serve, carefully remove side of pan; let stand 45 minutes before cutting into wedges. Garnish as desired.

Makes 8 main-dish or 24 appetizer servings

Honey Nut Brie

¼ cup honey
¼ cup coarsely chopped pecans
1 tablespoon brandy (optional)
1 wheel (14 ounces) Brie cheese (about 5-inch diameter)

Combine honey, pecans and brandy, if desired, in small bowl. Place cheese on large round ovenproof platter or 9-inch pie plate.

Bake in preheated 500°F oven 4 to 5 minutes or until cheese softens. Drizzle honey mixture over top of cheese. Bake 2 to 3 minutes longer or until topping is thoroughly heated. *Do not melt cheese.*

Makes 16 to 20 servings

Tip: Serve as a party dish with crackers, tart apple wedges and seedless grapes.

Holiday Meat and Vegetable Kabobs

- 1 cup fresh pearl onions
- ⅓ cup olive oil
- 2 tablespoons balsamic vinegar
- 1 tablespoon TABASCO® brand Pepper Sauce
- 1 tablespoon dried basil leaves
- 2 large cloves garlic, crushed
- 1 teaspoon salt
- 1 pound boneless skinless chicken breasts
- 1 pound boneless beef sirloin
- 2 large red peppers, cored, seeded and cut into ¾-inch pieces
- 1 large green pepper, cored, seeded and cut into ¾-inch pieces
- 1 large zucchini, cut into ¾-inch pieces

Soak 3 dozen 4-inch-long wooden skewers in water overnight. Bring pearl onions and enough water to cover in 1-quart saucepan over high heat to a boil. Reduce heat to low. Cover and simmer 3 minutes or until onions are tender. Drain. When cool enough to handle, peel away outer layer of skin from onions.

Combine oil, vinegar, TABASCO® Sauce, basil, garlic and salt in medium bowl. Pour half of mixture into another bowl. Cut chicken and beef into ¾-inch pieces and place in bowl with TABASCO® Sauce mixture, tossing well to coat. In remaining bowl of TABASCO® Sauce mixture, toss pearl onions, red and green peppers and zucchini. Let stand at least 30 minutes, tossing occasionally.

Preheat broiler. Skewer 1 piece of chicken or beef and 1 piece each of red pepper, green pepper, onion and zucchini onto each wooden pick. Broil 4 to 6 minutes, turning occasionally.

Makes 3 dozen hors d'oeuvres

Ginger-Lemon Cheese Spread with Pineapple-Peach Sauce

2 packages (8 ounces each) cream cheese, softened
1 cup sour cream
3 tablespoons packed brown sugar
1 tablespoon grated lemon peel
¾ teaspoon ground ginger
½ cup crushed pineapple, well drained
½ cup peach or apricot preserves
Assorted crackers and fresh fruit

1. Line 3-cup decorative mold or bowl with plastic wrap.

2. Combine cream cheese and sour cream in large bowl; beat until creamy. (Do not overbeat.) Add brown sugar, lemon peel and ginger; stir until well blended.

3. Spoon cheese mixture into prepared mold. Cover with plastic wrap; refrigerate at least 8 hours or up to 2 days.

4. To complete recipe, combine pineapple and peach preserves in small bowl. Unmold cheese spread onto serving plate. Spoon sauce around cheese. Serve with crackers and fresh fruit.

Makes 8 servings

Variation: Press toasted chopped walnuts onto cheese spread and serve Pineapple-Peach Sauce alongside of spread.

Serve It with Style!: Serve cheese spread with assorted crackers and apple and pear slices.

Make-Ahead Time: Up to 2 days before serving
Final Prep Time: 5 minutes

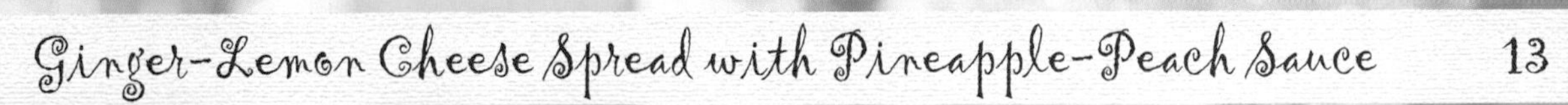

Festive Franks

1 can (8 ounces) reduced-fat crescent roll dough
5½ teaspoons barbecue sauce
⅓ cup finely shredded reduced-fat sharp Cheddar cheese
8 fat-free hot dogs
¼ teaspoon poppy seeds (optional)
Additional barbecue sauce (optional)

1. Preheat oven to 350°F. Spray large baking sheet with nonstick cooking spray; set aside.

2. Unroll dough and separate into 8 triangles. Cut each triangle in half lengthwise to make 2 triangles. Lightly spread barbecue sauce over each triangle. Sprinkle with cheese.

3. Cut each hot dog in half; trim off rounded ends. Place one hot dog piece at large end of one dough triangle. Roll up jelly-roll style from wide end. Place point-side down on prepared baking sheet. Sprinkle with poppy seeds, if desired. Repeat with remaining hot dog pieces and dough.

4. Bake 13 minutes or until dough is golden brown. Cool 1 to 2 minutes on baking sheet. Serve with additional barbecue sauce for dipping, if desired.

Makes 16 servings

Sausage Cheese Puffs

1 pound BOB EVANS® Original Recipe Roll Sausage
2½ cups (10 ounces) shredded sharp Cheddar cheese
2 cups biscuit mix
½ cup water
1 teaspoon baking powder

Preheat oven to 350°F. Combine ingredients in large bowl until blended. Shape into 1-inch balls. Place on lightly greased baking sheets. Bake about 25 minutes or until golden brown. Serve hot. Refrigerate leftovers. *Makes about 60 appetizers*

Chicken and Rice Puffs

1 box frozen puff pastry shells, thawed
1 package (about 6 ounces) long grain and wild rice
2 cups cubed cooked chicken
½ can (10¾ ounces) condensed cream of chicken soup, undiluted
⅓ cup chopped slivered almonds, toasted
⅓ cup diced celery
⅓ cup diced red bell pepper
⅓ cup chopped fresh parsley
¼ cup diced onion
¼ cup white wine or chicken broth
2 tablespoons half-and-half (optional)

1. Bake pastry shells according to package directions. Keep warm.

2. Prepare rice according to package directions.

3. Add remaining ingredients to rice; mix well. Cook 4 to 5 minutes until hot and bubbly. Fill pastry shells with rice mixture. Serve immediately. *Makes 6 servings*

Tip: This recipe is a great way to use up leftover chicken.

Artichoke and Crabmeat Party Dip

1 container (16 ounces) sour cream (2 cups)
1 packet (1 ounce) HIDDEN VALLEY® The Original Ranch® Dips Mix
1 can (14 ounces) artichoke hearts, rinsed, drained and chopped
¾ cup cooked crabmeat, rinsed and drained
2 tablespoons chopped red or green bell pepper
French bread slices, crackers or fresh vegetables, for dipping

Combine sour cream and dips mix. Stir in artichoke hearts, crabmeat and bell peppers. Chill 30 minutes. Serve with French bread, crackers or fresh vegetables.

Makes 3½ cups

Cheese Pine Cones

2 cups (8 ounces) shredded Swiss cheese
½ cup butter or margarine, softened
3 tablespoons milk
2 tablespoons dry sherry or milk
⅛ teaspoon ground red pepper
1 cup finely chopped blanched almonds
¾ cup slivered blanched almonds
¾ cup sliced almonds
½ cup whole almonds
Fresh rosemary sprigs
Assorted crackers

Beat cheese, butter, milk, sherry and red pepper in medium bowl until smooth; stir in chopped almonds.

Divide mixture into 3 equal portions; shape each into tapered ovals to resemble pine cones. Insert slivered, sliced and whole almonds into cones. Cover; refrigerate 2 to 3 hours or until firm.

Arrange Cheese Pine Cones on wooden board or serving plate. Garnish tops with rosemary. Serve with assorted crackers. *Makes 12 to 16 appetizer servings*

Crabmeat Spread

1 package (8 ounces) light cream cheese, softened
¼ cup cocktail sauce
1 package (8 ounces) imitation crabmeat

Spread cream cheese evenly on serving plate. Pour cocktail sauce over cream cheese; top with imitation crabmeat.

Serve with cocktail rye bread or assorted crackers. *Makes 1½ cups (12 servings)*

Prep Time: 5 minutes

Tri-Colored Tuna Stuffed Mushrooms

30 medium mushrooms, cleaned and stems removed
2 tablespoons melted butter or margarine
1 cup finely chopped onion
1 tablespoon vegetable oil
1 (3-ounce) pouch of STARKIST® Premium Albacore or Chunk Light Tuna
½ cup shredded smoked Gouda cheese, divided
1 red bell pepper, seeded and puréed*
1 package (10 ounces) frozen spinach soufflé
¼ cup mayonnaise, divided
¼ cup grated Parmesan cheese, divided
½ teaspoon curry powder

**To purée bell pepper: Place seeded and coarsely chopped red pepper in blender or food processor with metal blade. Blend or process until puréed.*

Lightly coat mushroom caps with melted butter; divide into 3 groups of 10. Sauté onion in hot oil until tender. In each of 3 small bowls, place 1/3 tuna and 1/3 sautéed onion. In first small bowl, add 1/4 cup Gouda cheese and red bell pepper purée.

In second small bowl, add 1/4 cup spinach soufflé,** 2 tablespoons mayonnaise, 2 tablespoons Parmesan cheese and curry powder. In third small bowl, add remaining 1/4 cup Gouda cheese, remaining 2 tablespoons mayonnaise and remaining 2 tablespoons Parmesan cheese. Fill 10 mushrooms with filling from each bowl. Arrange on baking sheet; bake in 350°F oven 10 to 12 minutes. Serve hot.

Makes 30 servings

***Keep remainder frozen until ready to use.*

Prep Time: 40 minutes

Cheesy Christmas Trees

½ cup mayonnaise
1 tablespoon dry ranch-style salad dressing mix
1 cup shredded Cheddar cheese
¼ cup grated Parmesan cheese
12 slices firm white bread
¼ cup red bell pepper strips
¼ cup green bell pepper strips

1. Preheat broiler. Combine mayonnaise and salad dressing mix in medium bowl. Add cheeses; mix well.

2. Cut bread slices into Christmas tree shapes using large cookie cutters. Spread each tree with about 1 tablespoon mayonnaise mixture. Decorate with red and green bell pepper strips. Place on baking sheet.

3. Broil 4 inches from heat 2 to 3 minutes or until bubbling. Serve warm.

Makes about 12 appetizers

Roast Beef Crostini with Spicy Horseradish Sauce

1 baguette French bread
½ cup mayonnaise
4 tablespoons prepared horseradish, drained
1 teaspoon TABASCO® brand Pepper Sauce
8 ounces roast beef, cooked medium rare, thinly sliced*
Fresh ground pepper

**Deli sliced roast beef may be substituted.*

Slice baguette into rounds ½ inch thick. Toast bread in toaster oven or broiler until light brown on both sides. Set aside.

Blend mayonnaise, horseradish and TABASCO® Sauce in small bowl. Spread generously on toast rounds. Top with roast beef slices; sprinkle with pepper.

Makes about 30 crostini

Barbecued Swedish Meatballs

Meatballs

1½ pounds lean ground beef
1 cup finely chopped onions
½ cup fresh breadcrumbs
½ cup HOLLAND HOUSE® White Cooking Wine
1 egg, beaten
½ teaspoon allspice
½ teaspoon nutmeg

Sauce

1 jar (10 ounces) currant jelly
½ cup chili sauce
¼ cup HOLLAND HOUSE® White Cooking Wine
1 tablespoon cornstarch

Heat oven to 350°F. In medium bowl, combine all meatball ingredients, mix well. Shape into 1-inch balls. Place meatballs in 15×10×1-inch baking pan. Bake 20 minutes or until brown.

In medium saucepan, combine all sauce ingredients; mix well. Cook over medium heat until mixture boils and thickens, stirring occasionally. Add meatballs. To serve, place meatballs and sauce in fondue pot or chafing dish. Sprinkle with chopped fresh parsley, if desired. Serve with cocktail picks.

Makes 6 to 8 servings

Festive Holiday Punch

8 cups MOTT'S® Apple Juice
8 cups cranberry juice cocktail
2 red apples, sliced
2 cups cranberries
3 liters lemon-lime soda
Ice cubes, as needed

Pour apple and cranberry juices into punch bowl. Fifteen minutes before serving, add apple slices, cranberries, soda and ice. Do not stir.

Makes 24 servings

Barbecued Swedish Meatballs

Cranberry-Glazed Brie

Ingredients

Cornmeal
¾ cup canned whole berry cranberry sauce, well drained
¼ teaspoon dry mustard
⅛ teaspoon ground ginger
⅛ teaspoon ground cloves
⅛ teaspoon ground allspice
1 package (17¼ ounces) frozen puff pastry sheets, thawed
1 round (15 ounces) fully ripened Brie cheese
1 egg
1 tablespoon water
Green, red and yellow food colors
Sliced pears and/or assorted crackers

Supplies

Small pastry brushes

1. Preheat oven to 400°F. Lightly sprinkle baking sheet with cornmeal.

2. Combine cranberry sauce, dry mustard and spices; mix well.

3. Place 1 puff pastry sheet on lightly floured surface; roll out pastry with rolling pin to a size about 2 inches larger than diameter of cheese round. Place cheese in center of pastry. With sharp knife, cut away excess pastry, leaving 1-inch rim around bottom of cheese; reserve trimmings. Place pastry and cheese on prepared baking sheet. Spread cranberry mixture onto top of cheese to within 1 inch of edge.

4. Roll out remaining pastry sheet to a size large enough to completely cover cheese. Place pastry over cheese; trim away excess pastry. (Be sure to leave 1-inch rim of pastry at bottom of cheese.) With sharp knife, cut slits in top of pastry to allow steam to vent.

5. Combine egg and water; beat lightly with fork. Brush onto pastry to cover completely. Fold up bottom rim of pastry; press edges together to seal.

6. Cut out leaf shapes or other decorative designs from pastry trimmings. "Glue" cutouts onto top of pastry-covered cheese with remaining egg mixture; brush with food colors that have been diluted slightly with water.

7. Bake 15 minutes. Reduce oven temperature to 350°F. Continue baking 15 to 20 minutes or until pastry is golden brown. Remove to wire rack; let stand 15 minutes before cutting to serve. Serve warm with pear slices or crackers.

Makes 12 appetizer servings

Festive Bacon & Cheese Dip

2 packages (8 ounces each) cream cheese, softened and cut into cubes
4 cups shredded Colby-Jack cheese
1 cup half-and-half
2 tablespoons prepared mustard
1 tablespoon chopped onion
2 teaspoons Worcestershire sauce
½ teaspoon salt
¼ teaspoon hot pepper sauce
1 pound bacon, cooked and crumbled

Slow Cooker Directions
Place cream cheese, Colby-Jack cheese, half-and-half, mustard, onion, Worcestershire sauce, salt and hot pepper sauce in slow cooker. Cover and cook, stirring occasionally, on LOW 1 hour or until cheese melts. Stir in bacon; adjust seasonings, if desired. Serve with crusty bread or fruit and vegetable dippers.

Makes about 1 quart

Beefy Stuffed Mushrooms

1 pound lean ground beef
2 teaspoons prepared horseradish
1 teaspoon chopped chives
1 clove garlic, minced
¼ teaspoon black pepper
18 large mushrooms
⅔ cup dry white wine

1. Thoroughly mix ground beef, horseradish, chives, garlic and pepper in medium bowl.

2. Remove stems from mushrooms; stuff mushroom caps with beef mixture.

3. Place stuffed mushrooms in shallow baking dish; pour wine over mushrooms. Bake in preheated 350°F oven until meat is browned, about 20 minutes.

Makes 1½ dozen appetizers

Mushrooms Rockefeller

18 large fresh button mushrooms (about 1 pound)
2 slices bacon
¼ cup chopped onion
1 package (10 ounces) frozen chopped spinach, thawed and squeezed dry
1 tablespoon lemon juice
1 teaspoon grated lemon peel
½ jar (2 ounces) chopped pimiento, drained
Lemon slices and lemon balm for garnish

1. Lightly spray 13×9-inch baking dish with nonstick cooking spray. Preheat oven to 375°F. Brush dirt from mushrooms; clean by wiping mushrooms with damp paper towel. Pull entire stem out of each mushroom cap; reserve.

2. Cut thin slice from base of each stem; discard. Chop remaining portions of stems.

3. Cook bacon in medium skillet over medium heat until crisp. Remove bacon with tongs to paper towel; set aside. Add mushroom stems and onion to hot drippings in skillet. Cook and stir until onion is soft. Add spinach, lemon juice, lemon peel and pimiento; blend well. Stuff mushroom caps with spinach mixture; place in single layer in prepared baking dish. Crumble reserved bacon and sprinkle on top of mushrooms. Bake 15 minutes or until heated through. Garnish, if desired. Serve immediately.

Makes 18 appetizers

Holiday Cheese Tree

Ingredients

2 cups (8 ounces) shredded Cheddar cheese
1 package (8 ounces) cream cheese, softened
3 tablespoons finely chopped red bell pepper
3 tablespoons finely chopped onion
1 tablespoon lemon juice
2 teaspoons Worcestershire sauce
¾ cup chopped fresh parsley
Red and yellow bell peppers

Supplies

Small (½- to ¾-inch) star-, tree- and bell-shaped cookie cutters

1. Combine cheeses, chopped bell pepper, onion, lemon juice and Worcestershire sauce in medium bowl; mix until well blended. Place on plate. Shape with hands to form cone shape, about 6 inches tall.

2. Press parsley evenly onto cheese tree.

3. Using cookie cutters, cut bell peppers into desired shapes. Press shapes onto tree for decorations.

4. Serve with assorted crackers and breadsticks.

Makes about 5 cups (14 to 16 appetizer servings)

Onion, Cheese and Tomato Tart

Parmesan-Pepper Dough (recipe follows)
1 tablespoon butter
1 medium onion, thinly sliced
1 cup (4 ounces) shredded Swiss cheese
2 to 3 ripe tomatoes, sliced
Black pepper
2 tablespoons snipped fresh chives

1. Make Parmesan-Pepper Dough. Set aside.

2. Melt butter in large skillet over medium heat. Add onion; cook and stir 20 minutes or until tender.

3. Spread onion over prepared dough. Sprinkle with cheese. Let rise in warm place 20 to 30 minutes or until edges are puffy.

4. Preheat oven to 400°F. Top dough with tomatoes. Sprinkle with pepper. Bake 25 minutes or until edges are deep golden and cheese is melted. Let cool 10 minutes. Transfer to serving platter. Sprinkle with chives. Cut into wedges.

Makes 6 to 8 servings

Parmesan-Pepper Dough

1 package (¼ ounce) active dry yeast
1 tablespoon sugar
⅔ cup warm water (105° to 115°F)
2 cups all-purpose flour, divided
¼ cup grated Parmesan cheese
1 teaspoon salt
½ teaspoon black pepper
1 tablespoon olive oil

1. Sprinkle yeast and sugar over warm water in small bowl; stir until yeast is dissolved. Let stand 5 minutes or until mixture is bubbly.

2. Combine 1¾ cups flour, cheese, salt and pepper in large bowl. Pour yeast mixture and oil over flour mixture and stir until mixture clings together.

3. Turn out dough onto lightly floured surface. Knead 8 to 10 minutes or until smooth and elastic, adding remaining ¼ cup flour if necessary. Shape dough into a ball; place in large greased bowl. Turn dough so that top is greased. Cover with towel; let rise in warm place 1 hour or until doubled in bulk.

4. Punch down dough. Knead on lightly floured surface 1 minute or until smooth. Flatten into a disc. Roll dough to make 11-inch round. Press into bottom and up side of buttered 9- or 10-inch tart pan with removable bottom.

Toasted Pesto Rounds

¼ cup thinly sliced fresh basil or chopped fresh dill
¼ cup (1 ounce) grated Parmesan cheese
1 medium clove garlic, minced
3 tablespoons reduced-calorie mayonnaise
12 French bread slices, about ¼ inch thick
4 teaspoons chopped tomato
1 green onion with top, sliced
Black pepper

1. Preheat broiler.

2. Combine basil, cheese, garlic and mayonnaise in small bowl; mix well.

3. Arrange bread slices in single layer on large nonstick baking sheet or broiler pan. Broil, 6 to 8 inches from heat, 30 to 45 seconds or until bread slices are lightly toasted.

4. Turn bread slices over; spread evenly with basil mixture. Broil 1 minute or until lightly browned. Top evenly with tomato and green onion. Season to taste with pepper. Transfer to serving plate.

Makes 12 servings

Herbed Stuffed Tomatoes

15 cherry tomatoes
½ cup 1% low-fat cottage cheese
1 tablespoon thinly sliced green onion
1 teaspoon chopped fresh chervil *or* ¼ teaspoon dried chervil leaves
½ teaspoon snipped fresh dill *or* ⅛ teaspoon dried dill weed
⅛ teaspoon lemon pepper

Cut thin slice off bottom of each tomato. Scoop out pulp with small spoon; discard pulp. Invert tomatoes on paper towels to drain.

Combine cottage cheese, green onion, chervil, dill and lemon pepper in small bowl. Spoon into tomatoes. Serve at once or cover and refrigerate up to 8 hours.

Makes 5 servings

Parmesan Polenta

4 cups chicken broth
1¼ cups yellow cornmeal
1 small onion, minced
4 cloves garlic, minced
1 tablespoon minced fresh rosemary *or* 1 teaspoon dried rosemary
½ teaspoon salt
6 tablespoons grated Parmesan cheese
1 tablespoon olive oil, divided

1. Spray 11×7-inch baking pan with nonstick cooking spray; set aside. Spray one side of 7-inch-long sheet of waxed paper with cooking spray; set aside. Combine chicken broth, cornmeal, onion, garlic, rosemary and salt in medium saucepan. Cover and bring to a boil over high heat. Reduce heat to medium and simmer 10 to 15 minutes or until mixture has consistency of thick mashed potatoes. Remove from heat and stir in cheese.

2. Spread polenta evenly in prepared pan; place waxed paper, sprayed-side down, on polenta and smooth. (If surface is bumpy, it is more likely to stick to grill.) Cool on wire rack 15 minutes or until firm. Remove waxed paper; cut into 6 squares. Remove squares from pan.

3. To prevent sticking, spray grid with cooking spray. Prepare coals for grilling. Brush tops of squares with half the oil. Grill oil-side down on covered grill over medium to low coals for 6 to 8 minutes or until golden. Brush with remaining oil and gently turn over. Grill 6 to 8 minutes more or until golden. Serve warm.

Nutty Bacon Cheeseball

1 package (8 ounces) cream cheese, softened
½ cup milk
2 cups (8 ounces) shredded sharp Cheddar cheese
2 cups (8 ounces) shredded Monterey Jack cheese
¼ cup (1 ounce) crumbled blue cheese
¼ cup finely minced green onions (white parts only)
1 jar (2 ounces) diced pimento, drained
10 slices bacon, cooked, drained, finely crumbled and divided
¾ cup finely chopped pecans, divided
Salt and black pepper to taste
¼ cup minced parsley
1 tablespoon poppy seeds

Beat cream cheese and milk on low speed in large bowl with electric mixer until blended. Add cheeses. Blend on medium speed until well combined. Add green onions, pimento, half of bacon and half of pecans. Blend on medium speed until well mixed. Add salt and pepper to taste. Transfer half of mixture to large piece of plastic wrap. Form into ball; wrap tightly. Repeat with remaining mixture. Refrigerate until chilled, at least two hours.

Combine remaining bacon and pecans with parsley and poppy seeds in pie plate or large dinner plate. Remove plastic wrap from each ball; roll each in bacon mixture until well coated. Wrap each ball tightly in plastic wrap and refrigerate until ready to use, up to 24 hours. Serve with assorted crackers or pita chips.

Makes about 24 servings

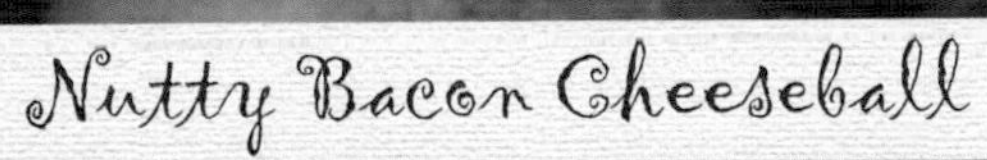

Nutty Bacon Cheeseball

Splendid Soups & Salads

Greens, White Bean and Barley Soup

½ pound carrots, peeled
2 tablespoons olive oil
1½ cups chopped onions
2 cloves garlic, minced
1½ cups sliced button mushrooms
3 cans (about 14½ ounces each) chicken broth
2 cups cooked barley
1 can (16 ounces) Great Northern beans, drained and rinsed
2 bay leaves
1 teaspoon sugar
1 teaspoon dried thyme leaves
1½ pounds collard greens, washed, stemmed and chopped (about 7 cups)
1 tablespoon white wine vinegar
Hot pepper sauce
Red bell pepper strips for garnish

Cut carrots lengthwise into quarters; cut crosswise into ¼-inch pieces. Heat oil in Dutch oven over medium heat until hot. Add carrots, onions and garlic; cook and stir 3 minutes. Add mushrooms; cook and stir 5 minutes or until tender.

Add broth, barley, beans, bay leaves, sugar and thyme. Bring to a boil over high heat. Reduce heat to low. Cover and simmer 5 minutes. Add greens; simmer 10 minutes. Remove bay leaves; discard. Stir in vinegar. Season to taste with pepper sauce. Garnish, if desired.

Makes 8 (1¼-cup) servings

Greens, White Bean and Barley Soup

Classic French Onion Soup

¼ cup butter
3 large yellow onions, sliced
1 cup dry white wine
3 cans (about 14 ounces each) beef or chicken broth
1 teaspoon Worcestershire sauce
½ teaspoon salt
½ teaspoon dried thyme
1 loaf French bread, sliced and toasted
1 cup (4 ounces) shredded Swiss cheese
Fresh thyme for garnish

Slow Cooker Directions
Melt butter in large skillet over high heat. Add onions, cook and stir 15 minutes or until onions are soft and lightly browned. Stir in wine.

Combine onion mixture, beef broth, Worcestershire, salt and thyme in slow cooker. Cover and cook on LOW 4 to 4½ hours. Ladle soup into 4 individual bowls; top with bread slice and cheese. Garnish with fresh thyme, if desired. *Makes 4 servings*

Pumpkin and Rice Soup

1 medium onion, chopped
1 clove garlic, minced
1 tablespoon vegetable oil
4 cups chicken broth
1 can (16 ounces) pumpkin
½ to 1 cup finely grated fresh pumpkin
½ teaspoon ground coriander
¼ to ½ teaspoon red pepper flakes
¼ teaspoon ground nutmeg
3 cups hot cooked rice
Cilantro sprigs for garnish

Cook onion and garlic in oil in large saucepan or Dutch oven over medium heat until onion is tender. Stir in broth, canned pumpkin, fresh pumpkin, coriander, pepper flakes and nutmeg. Bring to a boil. Reduce heat; simmer, uncovered, 5 to 10 minutes. Top each serving with ½ cup rice. Garnish with cilantro sprigs. *Makes 6 servings*

Favorite recipe from USA Rice Federation

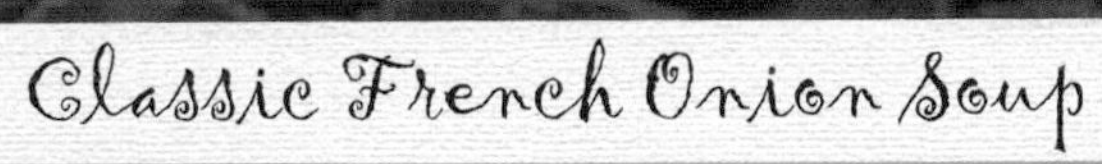

Hearty Lentil Stew

1 cup dried lentils, rinsed and drained
1 package (16 ounces) frozen green beans
2 cups cauliflower florets
1 cup chopped onion
1 cup baby carrots, cut in half crosswise
3 cups fat-free reduced-sodium chicken broth
2 teaspoons ground cumin
¾ teaspoon ground ginger
1 can (15 ounces) chunky tomato sauce with garlic and herbs
½ cup dry-roasted peanuts

Slow Cooker Directions

1. Place lentils in slow cooker. Top with green beans, cauliflower, onion and carrots. Combine broth, cumin and ginger in large bowl; mix well. Pour mixture over vegetables. Cover and cook on LOW 9 to 11 hours.

2. Stir in tomato sauce. Cover and cook on LOW 10 minutes. Ladle stew into bowls. Sprinkle peanuts evenly over each serving.

Makes 6 servings

Split Pea Soup

1 package (16 ounces) dried green or yellow split peas
1 pound smoked pork hocks *or* 4 ounces smoked sausage links, sliced and quartered *or* 1 meaty ham bone
7 cups water
1 medium onion, chopped
2 medium carrots, chopped
¾ teaspoon salt
½ teaspoon dried basil leaves
¼ teaspoon dried oregano leaves
¼ teaspoon black pepper
Ham and carrot strips for garnish

Rinse peas thoroughly in colander under cold running water, picking out any debris or blemished peas. Place peas, pork hocks and water in 5-quart Dutch oven.

Add onion, carrots, salt, basil, oregano and pepper to Dutch oven. Bring to a boil over high heat. Reduce heat to medium-low; simmer, uncovered, 1 hour 15 minutes or until peas are tender, stirring occasionally. Stir frequently near end of cooking to keep soup from scorching.

Remove pork hocks; cool. Cut meat into bite-size pieces.

Carefully ladle 3 cups hot soup into food processor or blender; cover and process until mixture is smooth.

Return puréed soup and meat to Dutch oven. (If soup is too thick, add a little water until desired consistency is reached.) Heat through. Ladle into bowls. Garnish, if desired.

Makes 6 servings

Mushroom-Beef Stew

1 pound beef stew meat
1 can (10¾ ounces) cream of mushroom soup, undiluted
1 envelope (1 ounce) dry onion soup mix
2 cans (4 ounces each) sliced mushrooms, drained

Slow Cooker Directions
Combine all ingredients in slow cooker. Cover and cook on LOW 8 to 10 hours.

Makes 4 servings

Serving Suggestion: Serve over hot cooked rice or noodles.

Ranch Clam Chowder

3 cans (6½ ounces each) chopped clams
6 slices bacon, chopped*
¼ cup finely chopped onion
¼ cup all-purpose flour
2½ cups milk
1 packet (1 ounce) HIDDEN VALLEY® The Original Ranch® Salad Dressing & Seasoning Mix
2 cups frozen cubed O'Brien potatoes
2 cups frozen corn kernels
⅛ teaspoon dried thyme (optional)

**Bacon pieces may be used.*

Drain clams, reserving juice (about 1⅓ cups); set aside. Cook bacon until crisp in a large pot or Dutch oven; remove with slotted spoon, reserving ¼ cup drippings.** Set aside bacon pieces. Heat bacon drippings over medium heat in same pot. Add onion; sauté 3 minutes. Sprinkle with flour; cook and stir 1 minute longer. Gradually whisk in reserved clam juice and milk, stirring until smooth. Whisk in salad dressing & seasoning mix until blended. Stir in potatoes, corn and thyme, if desired. Bring mixture just to a boil; reduce heat and simmer 10 minutes, stirring occasionally. Stir in clams; heat through. Sprinkle bacon on each serving. *Makes 4 to 6 servings*

***¼ cup butter may be used.*

Vegetable-Bean Chowder

½ cup chopped onion
½ cup chopped celery
2 cups water
½ teaspoon salt
2 cups cubed, peeled, potatoes
1 cup carrot slices
1 can (15 ounces) cream-style corn
1 can (15 ounces) cannellini beans or navy beans, drained and rinsed
¼ teaspoon dried tarragon leaves
¼ teaspoon black pepper
2 cups low-fat (1%) milk
2 tablespoons cornstarch

1. Spray 4-quart Dutch oven or large saucepan with nonstick cooking spray; heat over medium heat until hot. Add onion and celery. Cook and stir 3 minutes or until crisp-tender.

2. Add water and salt. Bring to a boil over high heat. Add potatoes and carrot. Reduce heat to medium. Simmer, covered, 10 minutes or until potatoes and carrot are tender.

3. Stir in corn, beans, tarragon and pepper. Simmer, covered, 10 minutes or until heated through.

4. Stir milk into cornstarch in medium bowl until smooth. Stir into vegetable mixture. Simmer, uncovered, until thickened.

Makes 5 (1½-cup) servings

Winter White Chili

½ pound boneless pork loin *or* 2 boneless pork chops, cut into ½-inch cubes
½ cup chopped onion
1 teaspoon vegetable oil
1 (16-ounce) can navy beans, drained
1 (16-ounce) can chick peas, drained
1 (16-ounce) can white kernel corn, drained
1 (14½-ounce) can chicken broth
1 cup cooked wild rice
1 (4-ounce) can diced green chilies, drained
1½ teaspoons ground cumin
¼ teaspoon garlic powder
⅛ teaspoon hot pepper sauce
Chopped parsley and shredded cheese
Shredded cheese

In 4-quart saucepan, sauté pork and onion in oil over medium-high heat until onion is soft and pork is lightly browned, about 5 minutes. Stir in remaining ingredients except parsley and shredded cheese. Cover and simmer for 20 minutes. Serve each portion garnished with parsley and shredded cheese. *Makes 6 servings*

Prep Time: 10 minutes
Cook Time: 25 minutes

Favorite recipe from National Pork Board

Cheddared Farmhouse Chowder

1 can (10½ ounces) condensed reduced-fat cream of mushroom soup
1½ cups fat-free milk or fat-free evaporated milk
1 bag (16 ounces) frozen corn, carrots and broccoli, thawed
2 medium baking potatoes, cut into ½-inch cubes
½ teaspoon dried thyme leaves
¼ teaspoon black pepper
⅛ teaspoon ground red pepper (optional)
½ cup frozen peas, thawed
¼ teaspoon salt
¾ cup (3 ounces) reduced-fat sharp Cheddar cheese, shredded

Combine soup and milk in large saucepan; whisk until well blended. Bring to a boil over medium-high heat, stirring frequently. Add vegetable mixture, potatoes, thyme, black pepper and ground red pepper, if desired. Return to a boil; reduce heat, cover, and simmer 15 minutes or until carrots are just tender, stirring frequently. Remove from heat; stir in peas and salt. Let stand 5 minutes for flavors to absorb. Ladle equal amounts into soup bowls. Top each with 3 tablespoons shredded cheese.

Makes 5 servings

Squash Bisque with Dill

2 boxes (12 ounces each) BIRDS EYE® frozen Cooked Winter Squash
2 cups skim milk, divided
1 tablespoon all-purpose flour
1 teaspoon dill weed
½ teaspoon chicken bouillon granules
Salt and pepper to taste

- In medium saucepan, cook squash according to package directions.
- Stir in 1 cup milk, flour, dill and bouillon.
- Cook over medium-high heat until heated through, stirring frequently. Season with salt and pepper.
- Stir in additional milk to obtain desired consistency; heat through.

Makes 4 servings

Prep Time: 2 minutes
Cook Time: 10 to 12 minutes

Turkey, Mandarin and Poppy Seed Salad

¼ cup orange juice
1½ tablespoons red wine vinegar
1½ teaspoons poppy seeds
1½ teaspoons olive oil
1 teaspoon Dijon-style mustard
⅛ teaspoon ground pepper
5 cups torn stemmed washed red leaf lettuce
2 cups torn stemmed washed spinach
½ pound honey roasted turkey breast, cut into ½-inch julienne strips
1 can (10½ ounces) mandarin oranges, drained

In small bowl, combine orange juice, vinegar, poppy seeds, oil, mustard and pepper. Set aside. In large bowl, toss together lettuce, spinach, turkey and oranges. Pour dressing over turkey mixture and serve immediately. *Makes 4 servings*

Favorite recipe from National Turkey Federation

Holiday Salad

1 head iceberg lettuce
1 bunch endive
½ pound cooked medium shrimp, shelled and deveined
1 can (12½ ounces) chunk white tuna, drained
1 cup whole pecans, toasted
3 hard-cooked eggs, chopped
1 cup prepared HIDDEN VALLEY® The Original Ranch® Dressing
2 tomatoes, cut into wedges

Wash, drain, then tear lettuce and endive into bite-size pieces; refrigerate. Layer one-third of lettuce-endive mixture in large bowl. Layer one-third of the shrimp, tuna, toasted pecans and eggs evenly over lettuce mixture. Repeat layers. Top with salad dressing. Cover and refrigerate until ready to serve. Toss before serving. Garnish with tomato wedges. *Makes 8 servings*

Pear and Cranberry Salad

½ cup canned whole berry cranberry sauce
2 tablespoons balsamic vinegar
1 tablespoon olive or canola oil
12 cups (9 ounces) packed assorted bitter or gourmet salad greens
6 small or 4 large pears (about 1¾ pounds)
2 ounces blue or Gorgonzola cheese, crumbled
Black pepper

1. Combine cranberry sauce, vinegar and oil in small bowl; mix well. (Dressing may be covered and refrigerated up to 2 days before serving.)

2. Arrange greens on six serving plates. Cut pears lengthwise into ½-inch-thick slices; cut core and seeds from each slice. Arrange pears attractively over greens. Drizzle cranberry dressing over pears and greens; sprinkle with cheese. Sprinkle with pepper to taste.

Makes 6 servings

Note: Be sure to use ripe pears. Forelles and Red Bartletts are particularly well suited for use in this salad.

Prep Time: 20 minutes

Holiday Fruit Salad

3 packages (3 ounces each) strawberry flavor gelatin
3 cups boiling water
2 ripe DOLE® Bananas
1 package (16 ounces) frozen strawberries
1 can (20 ounces) DOLE® Crushed Pineapple
1 package (8 ounces) cream cheese, softened
1 cup dairy sour cream or plain yogurt
¼ cup sugar
Crisp DOLE® Lettuce leaves

• In large bowl, dissolve gelatin in boiling water. Slice bananas into gelatin mixture. Add frozen strawberries and undrained crushed pineapple. Reserve half of the mixture at room temperature. Pour remaining mixture into 13×9-inch pan. Refrigerate 1 hour or until firm.

• In mixer bowl, beat cream cheese with sour cream and sugar; spread over chilled layer. Gently spoon reserved gelatin mixture on top. Refrigerate until firm, about 2 hours.

• Cut into squares; serve on lettuce-lined salad plates. Garnish with additional pineapple and mint leaves, if desired.

Makes 12 servings

Texas Citrus and Salad Greens with Raspberry Vinaigrette

1 head Boston lettuce
1 head radicchio
2 heads Belgian endive
2 to 3 Texas Red Grapefruit, sectioned
½ pint fresh raspberries
Mint for garnish
Raspberry Vinaigrette (recipe follows)

Wash greens and pat dry. Line 4 salad plates, alternating leaves of Boston lettuce and radiccio. Separate large leaves of Belgian endive and trim bottom of each leaf to V-shape. Arrange 5 endive leaves radiating from center in spoke design. Place grapefruit sections on top of endive and in between some of endive leaves. Sprinkle about ¼ cup raspberries in center of each plate and over greens. Garnish with mint. Serve with Raspberry Vinaigrette. *Makes 4 servings*

Favorite recipe from TexaSweet Citrus Marketing, Inc.

Raspberry Vinaigrette

3 tablespoons raspberry vinegar
2 tablespoons sugar
¾ teaspoon paprika
¼ teaspoon salt
⅓ cup salad oil
2 tablespoons chopped scallions

In small mixing bowl, combine all dressing ingredients and whisk until blended. Refrigerate any remaining dressing. *Makes about ⅔ cup*

Favorite recipe from TexaSweet Citrus Marketing, Inc.

Carrot Raisin Salad with Citrus Dressing

¾ cup reduced-fat sour cream
¼ cup nonfat milk
1 tablespoon honey
1 tablespoon orange juice concentrate
1 tablespoon lime juice
Peel of 1 medium orange, grated
¼ teaspoon salt
8 medium carrots, peeled and coarsely shredded (about 2 cups)
¼ cup raisins
⅓ cup chopped cashews

Combine sour cream, milk, honey, orange juice concentrate, lime juice, orange peel and salt in small bowl. Blend well and set aside.

Combine carrots and raisins in large bowl. Pour dressing over; toss to coat. Cover and refrigerate 30 minutes. Toss again before serving. Top with cashews.

Makes 8 servings

Christmas Cabbage Slaw

2 cups finely shredded green cabbage
2 cups finely shredded red cabbage
1 cup jícama strips
¼ cup diced green bell pepper
¼ cup thinly sliced green onions with tops
¼ cup vegetable oil
¼ cup lime juice
¾ teaspoon salt
⅛ teaspoon black pepper
2 tablespoons coarsely chopped fresh cilantro

Combine cabbages, jícama, bell pepper and onions in large bowl. Whisk oil, lime juice, salt and black pepper in small bowl until well blended. Stir in cilantro. Pour over cabbage mixture; toss lightly. Cover; refrigerate 2 to 6 hours for flavors to blend.

Makes 4 to 6 servings

Warm Ginger Almond Chicken Salad

Dressing

⅓ cup GRANDMA'S® Molasses
¼ cup oil
¼ cup cider vinegar
1 teaspoon finely chopped ginger root *or* ½ teaspoon ground ginger
1 teaspoon soy sauce
½ teaspoon salt
Dash hot pepper sauce

Salad

1 pound boneless, skinless chicken breasts, cut into thin strips
4 cups, torn mixed greens
1 cup (2 medium) shredded carrots
¼ cup chopped green onions
1 tablespoon cornstarch
2 tablespoons water
¼ cup sliced almonds, toasted

1. In medium bowl, combine all dressing ingredients. Add chicken strips; blend well. Cover; refrigerate 1 to 2 hours. In serving bowl, combine greens, carrots and green onions. Refrigerate.

2. In large skillet, combine chicken and dressing. Bring to a boil, cooking and stirring until chicken is no longer pink in center, about 3 to 5 minutes. In small bowl, combine cornstarch and water; blend well. Stir into chicken mixture. Cook until mixture thickens, stirring constantly. Spoon hot chicken mixture over vegetables; toss to combine. Sprinkle with almonds. Serve immediately. *Makes 4 servings*

Mixed Greens with Raspberry Vinaigrette

½ cup walnut halves
⅓ cup vegetable oil
2½ tablespoons raspberry vinegar
1 tablespoon chopped shallot
½ teaspoon salt
½ teaspoon sugar
2 cups washed and torn Romaine lettuce leaves
2 cups washed and torn spinach leaves
2 cups washed and torn red leaf lettuce leaves
1 cup halved red seedless grapes

Preheat oven to 350°F. To toast walnuts, spread in single layer on baking sheet. Bake 6 to 8 minutes or until lightly golden brown, stirring frequently; cool. Coarsely chop; set aside.

Place oil, vinegar, shallot, salt and sugar in small bowl or small jar with lid. Whisk together or cover and shake jar until mixed. Cover; refrigerate up to 1 week. Combine greens, grapes and chopped walnuts in large bowl. Just before serving, add dressing; toss well to coat.

Makes 6 to 8 servings

Orange-Onion Salad

1 tablespoon rice vinegar
1 tablespoon soy sauce
2 teaspoons dark sesame oil
1 large navel orange, peeled and sliced
1 small red onion, thinly sliced
Romaine lettuce or spinach leaves
Carrot curls for garnish

1. Combine vinegar, soy sauce and sesame oil in small bowl.

2. Place orange and onion slices in single layer in shallow baking dish; drizzle with soy sauce mixture. Cover and refrigerate at least 30 minutes or up to 8 hours.

3. Transfer orange and onion slices to lettuce-lined serving platter or individual lettuce-lined dishes; drizzle with juices from dish. Garnish with carrot curls.

Makes 4 servings

Mixed Greens with Raspberry Vinaigrette

Green Salad with Pears and Pecans

¼ cup reduced-fat mayonnaise
¼ cup reduced-fat sour cream
¾ tablespoon balsamic vinegar
1 tablespoon olive oil
1 tablespoon finely minced onion
⅛ teaspoon black pepper
Salt to taste
1 bag (10 ounces) mixed salad greens
2 ripe pears, cored and thinly sliced
1 cup (4 ounces) finely shredded Swiss cheese
½ cup pecans, toasted
Pomegranate seeds (optional)

Combine mayonnaise, sour cream, vinegar, oil, onion, pepper and salt in small bowl. Blend well and set aside.

Arrange greens evenly on four plates. Place pear slices around edges of plates. Sprinkle cheese and pecans over greens. Drizzle dressing evenly over salads. Garnish with pomegranate seeds, if desired. *Makes 4 servings*

Warm Potato & Bean Salad

16 small red new potatoes, halved
1 large green or red bell pepper, cut into 1-inch squares
3 tablespoons Italian dressing, divided
1 can (15 ounces) kidney or pinto beans, rinsed and drained
2 large green onions with tops, chopped
1 teaspoon dried parsley flakes

1. Prepare barbecue grill for direct cooking.

2. Place potatoes in large saucepan; cover with water. Bring potatoes to a boil over high heat. Cook 9 minutes or until barely fork-tender. Drain; rinse under cold running water.

3. Alternately thread potatoes and bell pepper on 4 long metal skewers, or place on vegetable grilling grid. Brush 2 tablespoons dressing evenly over vegetables.

4. Place skewers on barbecue grid. Grill, on covered grill, over hot coals 10 minutes or until potatoes are tender, turning skewers halfway through grilling time.

5. Meanwhile, combine remaining 1 tablespoon dressing, beans, green onions and parsley in large serving bowl. Remove vegetables from skewers into bowl; toss well. Serve immediately.
Makes 4 servings

Tip: Use canned whole white potatoes, cut into halves. No need to parboil; just skewer with bell pepper squares.

Prep and Cook Time: 22 minutes

Warm Chutney Chicken Salad

Nonstick olive oil cooking spray
6 ounces boneless skinless chicken breasts, cut into bite-size pieces
⅓ cup mango chutney
¼ cup water
1 tablespoon Dijon mustard
4 cups packaged mixed salad greens
1 cup chopped peeled mango or papaya
Sliced green onions (optional)

1. Spray medium nonstick skillet with cooking spray. Heat over medium-high heat. Add chicken; cook and stir 2 to 3 minutes or until no longer pink. Stir in chutney, water and mustard. Cook and stir just until hot. Cool slightly.

2. Toss together salad greens and mango. Arrange on serving plates.

3. Spoon chicken mixture onto greens. Garnish with green onions, if desired.

Makes 2 servings

Caramelized Apple & Onion Salad

¼ cup I CAN'T BELIEVE IT'S NOT BUTTER!® Spread
1 large Granny Smith or other tart apple, peeled, cored and thinly sliced
1 large onion, sliced
4 cups mixed salad greens or mesclun
WISH-BONE® Balsamic Vinaigrette Dressing
½ cup toasted chopped walnuts or pecans (optional)

In 12-inch skillet, melt I Can't Believe It's Not Butter!® Spread over medium-high heat and cook apple and onion, stirring occasionally, 4 minutes or until tender. Reduce heat to medium and cook uncovered, stirring occasionally, 20 minutes or until apple and onion are golden brown. Serve warm apple mixture over greens. Drizzle with dressing and garnish with walnuts.

Makes 2 servings

Heartwarming Breads

Pumpkin Bread

1 package (about 18 ounces) yellow cake mix
1 can (16 ounces) solid pack pumpkin
⅓ cup GRANDMA'S® Molasses
4 eggs
1 teaspoon cinnamon
1 teaspoon nutmeg
⅓ cup nuts, chopped (optional)
⅓ cup raisins (optional)

Preheat oven to 350°F. Grease two 9×5-inch loaf pans.

Combine all ingredients in a large bowl and mix well. Beat at medium speed 2 minutes. Pour into prepared pans. Bake 60 minutes or until toothpick inserted into center comes out clean.

Makes 2 loaves

Hint: Serve with cream cheese or preserves, or top with cream cheese frosting or ice cream.

Potato Rosemary Rolls

Dough

1 cup plus 2 tablespoons water (70° to 80°F)
2 tablespoons olive oil
1 teaspoon salt
3 cups bread flour
½ cup instant potato flakes or buds
2 tablespoons nonfat dry milk powder
1 tablespoon sugar
1 teaspoon SPICE ISLANDS® Rosemary, crushed
1½ teaspoons FLEISCHMANN'S® Bread Machine Yeast

Topping

1 egg, lightly beaten
Sesame or poppy seeds or additional dried rosemary, crushed

Measure all dough ingredients into bread machine pan in the order suggested by manufacturer, adding potato flakes with flour. Select dough/manual cycle. When cycle is complete, remove dough to floured surface. If necessary, knead in additional flour to make dough easy to handle.

Divide dough into 12 equal pieces. Roll each piece to 10-inch rope; coil each rope and tuck end under coil. Place rolls 2 inches apart on large greased baking sheet. Cover; let rise in warm, draft-free place until doubled in size, about 45 to 60 minutes. Brush tops with beaten egg; sprinkle with sesame seeds. Bake at 375°F for 15 to 20 minutes or until done. Remove from pan; cool on wire rack.

Makes 12 rolls

Note: Dough can be prepared in 1½ and 2-pound bread machines.

Cranberry Raisin Nut Bread

1½ cups all-purpose flour
¾ cup packed light brown sugar
1½ teaspoons baking powder
½ teaspoon baking soda
½ teaspoon ground cinnamon
½ teaspoon ground nutmeg
1 cup coarsely chopped fresh or frozen cranberries
½ cup golden raisins
½ cup coarsely chopped pecans
1 tablespoon grated orange peel
¾ cup milk
2 eggs
3 tablespoons butter, melted
1 teaspoon vanilla
Cranberry-Orange Spread (recipe follows, optional)

Preheat oven to 350°F. Grease 8½×4½-inch loaf pan.

Combine flour, brown sugar, baking powder, baking soda, cinnamon and nutmeg in large bowl. Stir in cranberries, raisins, pecans and orange peel. Mix milk, eggs, butter and vanilla in small bowl until combined; stir into flour mixture just until moistened. Spoon into prepared pan.

Bake 55 to 60 minutes or until wooden toothpick inserted into center comes out clean. Cool in pan 15 minutes. Remove from pan and cool completely on wire rack. Store tightly wrapped in plastic wrap at room temperature. Serve slices with Cranberry-Orange Spread, if desired.

Makes 1 loaf

Cranberry-Orange Spread

1 package (8 ounces) cream cheese, softened
1 package (3 ounces) cream cheese, softened
1 container (12 ounces) cranberry-orange sauce
¾ cup chopped pecans

Combine cream cheese and cranberry-orange sauce in small bowl; stir until blended. Stir in pecans. Store in refrigerator.

Makes about 3 cups spread

Cranberry Cheesecake Muffins

1 package (3 ounces) cream cheese, softened
4 tablespoons sugar, divided
1 cup reduced-fat (2%) milk
⅓ cup vegetable oil
1 egg
1 package (about 15 ounces) cranberry quick bread mix

1. Preheat oven to 400°F. Grease 12 muffin cups.

2. Beat cream cheese and 2 tablespoons sugar in small bowl until well blended.

3. Beat milk, oil and egg in large bowl until blended. Stir in quick bread mix just until dry ingredients are moistened.

4. Fill muffin cups 1/4 full with batter. Drop 1 teaspoon cream cheese mixture into center of each cup. Spoon remaining batter over cream cheese mixture.

5. Sprinkle batter with remaining 2 tablespoons sugar. Bake 17 to 22 minutes or until golden brown. Cool 5 minutes. Remove from muffin cups to wire rack to cool.

Makes 12 muffins

Prep and Bake Time: 30 minutes

Festive Yule Loaf

2¾ cups all-purpose flour, divided
⅓ cup sugar
1 teaspoon salt
1 package active dry yeast
1 cup milk
½ cup butter or margarine
1 egg
½ cup golden raisins
½ cup chopped candied red and green cherries
½ cup chopped pecans
Vanilla Glaze (recipe follows, optional)

Combine 1½ cups flour, sugar, salt and yeast in large bowl. Heat milk and butter over medium heat until very warm (120° to 130°F). Gradually stir into flour mixture. Add egg. Mix with electric mixer on low speed 1 minute. Beat on high speed 3 minutes, scraping sides of bowl frequently. Toss raisins, cherries and pecans with ¼ cup flour in small bowl; stir into yeast mixture. Stir in enough of remaining 1 cup flour to make a soft dough. Turn out onto lightly floured surface. Knead about 10 minutes or until smooth and elastic. Place in greased bowl; turn to grease top of dough. Cover with towel. Let rise in warm, draft-free place about 1 hour or until double in volume.

Punch dough down. Divide in half. Roll out each half on lightly floured surface to form 8-inch circle. Fold in half; press only folded edge firmly. Place on ungreased cookie sheet. Cover with towel. Let rise in warm, draft-free place about 30 minutes or until double in volume.

Preheat oven to 375°F. Bake 20 to 25 minutes until golden brown. Remove from cookie sheet and cool completely on wire rack. Frost with Vanilla Glaze, if desired. Store in airtight containers. *Makes 2 loaves*

Vanilla Glaze: Combine 1 cup sifted powdered sugar, 4 to 5 teaspoons light cream or half-and-half and ½ teaspoon vanilla extract in small bowl; stir until smooth.

Pull-Apart Rye Rolls

¾ cup water
2 tablespoons margarine or butter, softened
2 tablespoons molasses
2¼ cups all-purpose flour, divided
½ cup rye flour
⅓ cup nonfat dry milk powder
1 package active dry yeast
1½ teaspoons salt
1½ teaspoons caraway seeds
Melted margarine or vegetable oil

Heat water, margarine and molasses in small saucepan over low heat until temperature reaches 120° to 130°F. Combine 1¼ cups all-purpose flour, rye flour, milk powder, yeast, salt and caraway seeds in large bowl. Stir heated water mixture into flour mixture with wooden spoon to form soft but sticky dough. Gradually add more all-purpose flour until rough dough forms.

Turn out dough onto lightly floured surface. Knead 5 to 8 minutes or until smooth and elastic, gradually adding remaining flour to prevent sticking, if necessary. Cover with inverted bowl. Let rise 35 to 40 minutes or until dough has increased in bulk by one third. Punch down dough; divide into halves. Roll each half into 12-inch log. Cut each log evenly into 12 pieces using sharp knife; shape into tight balls. Arrange in greased 8- or 9-inch cake pan. Brush tops with melted margarine. Loosely cover with lightly greased sheet of plastic wrap. Let rise in warm place 45 minutes or until doubled in bulk.

Preheat oven to 375°F. Uncover rolls; bake 15 to 20 minutes or until golden brown. Cool in pan on wire rack 5 minutes. Remove from pan. Cool completely on wire rack.

Makes 24 rolls

Cherry Eggnog Quick Bread

2½ cups all-purpose flour
¾ cup sugar
1 tablespoon baking powder
½ teaspoon ground nutmeg
1¼ cups prepared dairy eggnog
6 tablespoons butter, melted and cooled
2 eggs, lightly beaten
1 teaspoon vanilla
½ cup chopped pecans
½ cup chopped candied red cherries

Preheat oven to 350°F. Grease three 5½×3-inch mini-loaf pans.

Combine flour, sugar, baking powder and nutmeg in large bowl. Stir eggnog, melted butter, eggs and vanilla in medium bowl until well blended. Add eggnog mixture to flour mixture. Mix just until all ingredients are moistened. Stir in pecans and cherries. Spoon into prepared pans.

Bake 35 to 40 minutes or until wooden toothpick inserted in centers comes out clean. Cool in pans 15 minutes. Remove from pans and cool completely on wire rack. Store tightly wrapped in plastic wrap at room temperature. *Makes 3 mini loaves*

Cinnamon Sugared Pumpkin-Pecan Muffins

½ cup granulated sugar, divided
2½ to 3 teaspoons ground cinnamon, divided
1 cup 100% bran cereal
1 cup fat-free (skim) milk
1 cup all-purpose flour
1 tablespoon baking powder
½ teaspoon baking soda
½ teaspoon salt
1 cup canned pumpkin
1 egg, beaten
1 tablespoon vanilla extract
1 package (2 ounces) pecan chips

Preheat oven to 400°F. Coat nonstick 12-cup muffin pan with nonstick cooking spray. Combine 2 tablespoons sugar and ½ to 1 teaspoon cinnamon in small bowl for topping; set aside.

Blend cereal and milk in large bowl; set aside 5 minutes to soften. Meanwhile, combine flour, remaining sugar and cinnamon, baking powder, baking soda and salt in large bowl; mix well.

Whisk pumpkin, egg and vanilla into softened cereal. Gently fold in flour mixture just until blended. *Do not overmix.* Spoon equal amounts of batter into each muffin cup; sprinkle evenly with pecan chips. Sprinkle with reserved cinnamon-sugar topping.

Bake 20 to 25 minutes. Cool on wire rack 3 minutes before removing muffins from pan. Serve warm or at room temperature. *Makes 12 servings*

Whole Wheat Herbed Bread Wreath

4 cups all-purpose flour, divided
2 packages active dry yeast
2 tablespoons sugar
4 teaspoons dried rosemary
1 tablespoon salt
2½ cups water
2 tablespoons olive oil
3 cups whole wheat flour, divided
1 egg, beaten

Combine 2½ cups all-purpose flour, yeast, sugar, rosemary and salt in large bowl. Heat water until very warm (120° to 130°F). Gradually add water and oil to flour mixture until blended. Beat with electric mixer on medium speed 2 minutes. Add 1 cup whole wheat flour. Beat on high speed 2 minutes, scraping sides of bowl occasionally. By hand, stir in enough of remaining flours to make a soft, sticky dough. Place in greased bowl; turn to grease top of dough. Cover with towel. Let rise in warm, draft-free place about 1½ hours or until doubled in volume.

Punch down dough. Turn out onto well-floured surface. Knead about 10 minutes or until smooth and elastic. Divide into thirds. Roll each piece to form 24-inch rope. Place on large greased cookie sheet. Braid ropes beginning at center and working toward ends. Seal edges. Shape into circle around greased 10-ounce ovenproof round bowl. Seal ends well. Cover with towel. Let rise in warm, draft-free place about 30 minutes or until doubled in volume.

Preheat oven to 450°F. Carefully brush wreath with egg. Bake 25 to 30 minutes until wreath sounds hollow when tapped and top is golden brown. Cool on cookie sheet 10 minutes. Carefully remove from cookie sheet and bowl; cool completely on wire rack. Store tightly wrapped in plastic wrap at room temperature.

Makes one 12-inch wreath

Tip: If desired, fill center of bread with watercress radish roses and star shaped cutouts of flavored cheese.

Holiday Rye Bread

3 to 3½ cups all-purpose flour
2½ cups rye flour
⅓ cup sugar
2 envelopes FLEISCHMANN'S® RapidRise™ Yeast
2½ teaspoons salt
1 tablespoon grated orange peel
2 teaspoons fennel seed
1 cup beer or malt liquor
½ cup water
¼ cup light molasses
2 tablespoons butter or margarine
Molasses Glaze (recipe follows)

In large bowl, combine 1½ cups all-purpose flour, rye flour, sugar, undissolved yeast, salt, orange peel, and fennel seed. Heat beer, water, molasses, and butter until very warm (120° to 130°F). Stir into dry ingredients. Beat 2 minutes at medium speed of electric mixer, scraping bowl occasionally. Stir in enough remaining flour to make soft dough. Knead on lightly floured surface until smooth and elastic, about 8 to 10 minutes. Cover; let rest 10 minutes.

Divide dough into 4 equal pieces. Roll each to 10×6-inch oval. Roll each up tightly from long side, as for jelly roll, tapering ends. Pinch seams to seal. Place on greased baking sheets. Cover; let rise in warm, draft-free place until doubled in size, about 1½ hours.

With sharp knife, make 3 diagonal cuts on top of each loaf. Brush with Molasses Glaze. Bake at 375°F for 15 minutes; brush loaves with Glaze. Bake additional 10 minutes or until done. Remove loaves from oven and brush again with Glaze. Cool on wire racks. *Makes 4 small loaves*

Molasses Glaze: Combine 2 tablespoons molasses and 2 tablespoons water. Stir until well blended.

Pumpkin-Ginger Scones

½ cup sugar, divided
2 cups all-purpose flour
2 teaspoons baking powder
1 teaspoon ground cinnamon
½ teaspoon baking soda
½ teaspoon salt
5 tablespoons butter, divided
1 egg
½ cup solid pack pumpkin
¼ cup sour cream
½ teaspoon grated fresh ginger *or* 2 tablespoons finely chopped crystallized ginger

Preheat oven to 425°F.

Reserve 1 tablespoon sugar. Combine remaining sugar, flour, baking powder, cinnamon, baking soda and salt in large bowl. Cut in 4 tablespoons butter with pastry blender until mixture resembles coarse crumbs. Beat egg in small bowl. Add pumpkin, sour cream and ginger; beat until well combined. Add pumpkin mixture to flour mixture; stir until mixture forms soft dough that leaves side of bowl.

Turn dough out onto well-floured surface. Knead 10 times. Roll dough using floured rolling pin into 9×6-inch rectangle. Cut dough into 6 (3-inch) squares. Cut each square diagonally in half, making 12 triangles. Place triangles, 2 inches apart, on ungreased baking sheets. Melt remaining 1 tablespoon butter. Brush tops of triangles with butter and sprinkle with reserved sugar.

Bake 10 to 12 minutes or until golden brown. Cool 10 minutes on wire racks. Serve warm.

Makes 12 scones

Apricot Holiday Bread

- **⅔ cup milk**
- **1 egg**
- **2 tablespoons butter, softened**
- **1 teaspoon salt**
- **3 cups all-purpose flour**
- **2 tablespoons sugar**
- **½ cup pecan or walnut pieces**
- **½ cup dried apricots or peaches, chopped**
- **1 tablespoon active dry yeast**
- **¼ teaspoon ground ginger**
- **¼ teaspoon ground nutmeg**

1. Measuring carefully, place all ingredients in bread machine pan in order specified by owner's manual.

2. Program basic or white cycle and desired crust setting; press start. *(Do not use delay cycle.)* Remove baked bread from pan; cool on wire rack.

Makes 1 (1½-pound) loaf (12 to 16 servings)

Cranberry Pecan Wreath

3½ to 4 cups all-purpose flour
⅓ cup sugar
1 envelope FLEISCHMANN'S® RapidRise™ Yeast
¾ teaspoon salt
½ cup milk
⅓ cup butter or margarine
¼ cup water
2 large eggs
Cranberry-Pecan Filling (recipe follows)
Orange Glaze (recipe follows)

In large bowl, combine 1½ cups flour, sugar, undissolved yeast and salt. Heat milk, butter and water until very warm (120° to 130°F); stir into dry ingredients. Stir in eggs and enough remaining flour to make soft dough. Knead on lightly floured surface until smooth and elastic, about 8 to 10 minutes. Cover; let rest 10 minutes.

Roll dough to 30×6-inch rectangle; spread Cranberry-Pecan Filling over dough to within ½ inch of edges. Beginning at long end, roll up tightly, pinching seam to seal. Form into ring; join ends, pinching to seal. Transfer to greased large baking sheet. Cover; let rise in warm, draft-free place until doubled in size, about 45 to 60 minutes.

Bake at 350°F for 40 to 45 minutes or until done. Remove from pan; cool on wire rack. Drizzle with Orange Glaze. Decorate with additional cranberries, orange slices and pecan halves, if desired.

Makes 1 (10-inch) coffeecake

Cranberry-Pecan Filling: In medium saucepan, combine 1½ cups fresh or frozen cranberries, finely chopped; 1 cup firmly packed brown sugar; and ⅓ cup butter or margarine. Bring to a boil over medium-high heat. Reduce heat; simmer 5 to 7 minutes or until very thick, stirring frequently. Remove mixture from heat; stir in ¾ cup chopped pecans, toasted.

Orange Glaze: In small bowl, combine 1¼ cups sifted powdered sugar; 2 tablespoons butter or margarine, softened; 1 to 2 tablespoons milk; and 2 teaspoons freshly grated orange peel. Stir until smooth.

Satisfying Side Dishes

Golden Apples and Yams

2 large yams or sweet potatoes
2 Washington Golden Delicious apples, cored and sliced crosswise into rings
¼ cup firmly packed brown sugar
1 teaspoon cornstarch
⅛ teaspoon ground cloves
½ cup orange juice
2 tablespoons chopped pecans or walnuts

Heat oven to 400°F. Bake yams 50 minutes or until soft but still hold their shape. (This can also be done in microwave.) Let yams cool enough to handle. *Reduce oven to 350°F.*

Peel and slice yams crosswise. In shallow 1-quart baking dish, alternate apple rings and yam slices, overlapping edges slightly. In small saucepan, combine sugar, cornstarch and cloves; stir in orange juice and mix well. Heat orange juice mixture over medium heat, stirring, until thickened; pour over apples and yams. Sprinkle with nuts; bake 20 minutes or until apples and yams are tender. *Makes 6 servings*

Favorite recipe from **Washington Apple Commission**

Golden Apples and Yams

Green Beans with Toasted Pecans

3 tablespoons I CAN'T BELIEVE IT'S NOT BUTTER!® Spread, melted
1 teaspoon sugar
¼ teaspoon garlic powder
Pinch ground red pepper
Salt to taste
⅓ cup chopped pecans
1 pound green beans

In small bowl, blend I Can't Believe It's Not Butter! Spread, sugar, garlic powder, pepper and salt.

In 12-inch nonstick skillet, heat 2 teaspoons garlic mixture over medium-high heat and cook pecans, stirring frequently, 2 minutes or until pecans are golden. Remove pecans and set aside.

In same skillet, heat remaining garlic mixture and stir in green beans. Cook, covered, over medium heat, stirring occasionally, 6 minutes or until green beans are tender. Stir in pecans.

Makes 4 servings

Festive Cranberry Mold

½ cup water
1 package (6 ounces) raspberry-flavored gelatin
1 can (8 ounces) cranberry sauce
1⅔ cups cranberry juice cocktail
1 cup sliced bananas (optional)
½ cup walnuts, toasted (optional)

In medium saucepan over medium-high heat, bring water to a boil. Add gelatin and stir until dissolved. Fold in cranberry sauce. Reduce heat to medium and cook until sauce is melted. Stir in cranberry juice cocktail.

Refrigerate mixture until slightly thickened. Fold in banana slices and walnuts, if desired. Pour mixture into 4-cup mold; cover and refrigerate until gelatin is set.

Makes 8 servings

Fruited Wild Rice with Toasted Nuts

2 boxes (6.2 ounces each) fast-cooking long grain and wild rice
2 tablespoons walnut or vegetable oil, divided
1 package (2½ ounces) walnut pieces *or* ⅔ cup almond slivers
1 package (2¼ ounces) pecan pieces
2 cups chopped onions
12 dried apricots, sliced (about ½ cup)
½ cup dried cherries or dried cranberries
2 teaspoons minced fresh ginger
¼ teaspoon red pepper flakes
¼ cup honey
3 tablespoons soy sauce
1 tablespoon grated orange peel

1. Cook rice according to package directions.

2. Meanwhile, add 1 tablespoon oil to large nonstick skillet or wok. Heat skillet over medium-high heat 1 minute. Add walnuts and pecans; cook, stirring frequently, 8 minutes or until pecans are browned. Remove from skillet and set aside.

3. Add remaining 1 tablespoon oil and onions to skillet; cook 10 minutes or until onions begin to brown. Add apricots, cherries, ginger, pepper flakes and reserved nuts; cook 5 minutes.

4. Whisk together honey, soy sauce and orange peel in small bowl; add to onion mixture. Toss with rice. *Makes 4 servings*

Note: This dish can be served as a chilled rice salad. Spoon hot cooked rice evenly on large baking sheet to cool quickly, about 8 to 10 minutes. Toss with cooled nuts, onion mixture and honey mixture.

Roasted Butternut Squash

- 1 pound butternut squash, peeled and cut into 1-inch cubes (about 4 cups)
- 2 medium onions, coarsely chopped
- 8 ounces carrots, peeled and cut into ½-inch diagonal slices (about 2 cups)
- 1 tablespoon dark brown sugar
- ¼ teaspoon salt
- Black pepper to taste
- 1 tablespoon butter or margarine, melted

Preheat oven to 400°F. Line large baking sheet with foil and coat with nonstick cooking spray. Arrange vegetables in single layer on foil; coat lightly with cooking spray. Sprinkle vegetables with brown sugar, salt and pepper.

Bake 30 minutes. Stir gently; bake 10 to 15 minutes longer or until vegetables are tender. Remove from oven; drizzle with butter and toss to coat.

Makes 5 (1-cup) servings

Green Bean Casserole

- 2 packages (10 ounces each) frozen green beans, thawed
- 1 can (10½ ounces) condensed cream of mushroom soup, undiluted
- 1 tablespoon chopped fresh parsley
- 1 tablespoon chopped roasted red peppers
- 1 teaspoon dried sage
- ½ teaspoon salt
- ½ teaspoon black pepper
- ¼ teaspoon ground nutmeg
- ½ cup toasted slivered almonds

Slow Cooker Directions

Combine all ingredients except almonds in slow cooker. Cover and cook on LOW 3 to 4 hours. Sprinkle with almonds.

Makes 4 to 6 servings

Rosemary-Garlic Mashed Potatoes

Roasted Garlic (recipe follows), mashed
2½ pounds Yukon Gold potatoes (5 medium), peeled and cut into 1-inch pieces
1½ teaspoons salt, divided
½ cup whipping cream or half-and-half
½ cup milk
2 tablespoons butter
1 tablespoon minced fresh rosemary *or* 1 teaspoon dried rosemary
⅛ teaspoon white pepper

Prepare Roasted Garlic.

Place potato pieces in medium saucepan; add water to cover and 1 teaspoon salt. Bring to a boil. Reduce heat and simmer, uncovered, about 12 to 15 minutes or until potatoes are tender. Drain potatoes and set aside.

Place cream, milk, butter and rosemary in small saucepan; heat over medium-high heat about 3 minutes or until butter melts and mixture simmers, stirring often. Mash potatoes with potato masher until smooth. Add Roasted Garlic and milk mixture; beat with electric mixer until smooth. Beat in remaining ½ teaspoon salt and pepper. Serve hot.

Makes 4 to 6 servings

Roasted Garlic: Cut off top third of 1 large garlic head to expose cloves; discard top. Place head of garlic, trimmed end up, on 10-inch square of foil. Rub garlic generously with olive oil and sprinkle with salt. Gather foil ends together and close tightly. Roast in preheated 350°F oven 45 minutes or until cloves are golden and soft. When cool enough to handle, squeeze roasted garlic cloves from skins; discard skins.

Sautéed Snow Peas & Baby Carrots

1 tablespoon I CAN'T BELIEVE IT'S NOT BUTTER!® Spread
2 tablespoons chopped shallots or onion
5 ounces frozen whole baby carrots, partially thawed
4 ounces snow peas (about 1 cup)
2 teaspoons chopped fresh parsley (optional)

In 12-inch nonstick skillet, melt I Can't Believe It's Not Butter! Spread over medium heat and cook shallots, stirring occasionally, 1 minute or until almost tender. Add carrots and snow peas and cook, stirring occasionally, 4 minutes or until crisp-tender. Stir in parsley and heat through. *Makes 2 servings*

Note: Recipe can be doubled.

Creamed Spinach à la Lawry's®

4 bacon slices, finely chopped
1 cup finely chopped onions
¼ cup all-purpose flour
2 teaspoons LAWRY'S® Seasoned Salt
½ teaspoon LAWRY'S® Seasoned Pepper
½ teaspoon LAWRY'S® Garlic Powder with Parsley
1½ to 2 cups milk
2 packages (10 ounces each) frozen spinach, cooked and drained

In medium skillet, fry bacon until almost crisp. Add onions to bacon and cook until onions are tender, about 10 minutes. Remove from heat. Add flour, Seasoned Salt, Seasoned Pepper and Garlic Powder with Parsley; mix well. Gradually add milk, starting with 1½ cups, and stir over low heat until thickened. Add spinach and mix thoroughly. If too thick, add additional milk. *Makes 8 servings*

Serving Suggestion: Serve with prime ribs of beef.

Sweet Potato Gratin

3 pounds sweet potatoes (about 5 large)
½ cup butter or margarine, divided
¼ cup plus 2 tablespoons packed light brown sugar, divided
2 eggs
⅔ cup orange juice
2 teaspoons ground cinnamon, divided
½ teaspoon salt
¼ teaspoon ground nutmeg
⅓ cup all-purpose flour
¼ cup uncooked old-fashioned oats
⅓ cup chopped pecans or walnuts

1. Preheat oven to 350°F. Bake sweet potatoes about 1 hour or until tender. Or, pierce sweet potatoes several times with table fork and place on microwavable plate. Microwave at HIGH 16 to 18 minutes, rotating and turning over potatoes after 9 minutes. Let stand 5 minutes.

2. Cut hot sweet potatoes lengthwise into halves. Scrape hot pulp from skins into large bowl.

3. Beat ¼ cup butter and 2 tablespoons sugar into sweet potatoes with electric mixer at medium speed until butter is melted. Add eggs, orange juice, 1½ teaspoons cinnamon, salt and nutmeg. Beat until smooth. Pour mixture into 1½-quart baking dish or gratin dish; smooth top.

4. For topping, combine flour, oats, remaining ¼ cup sugar and remaining ½ teaspoon cinnamon in medium bowl. Cut in remaining ¼ cup butter until mixture resembles coarse crumbs. Stir in pecans. Sprinkle topping evenly over sweet potatoes.*

5. Bake 25 to 30 minutes or until sweet potatoes are heated through. For crisper topping, broil 5 inches from heat 2 to 3 minutes or until golden brown.

Makes 6 to 8 servings

**At this point, Sweet Potato Gratin may be covered and refrigerated up to 1 day. Let stand at room temperature 1 hour before baking.*

Wild Rice Mushroom Stuffing

½ cup uncooked wild rice
Day-old French bread (about 4 ounces)
½ cup butter or margarine
1 large onion, chopped
1 clove garlic, minced
3 cups sliced fresh mushrooms*
½ teaspoon rubbed sage
½ teaspoon dried thyme leaves
½ teaspoon salt
¼ teaspoon black pepper
1 cup chicken broth
½ cup coarsely chopped pecans
Thyme sprigs for garnish

**Or, substitute 1½ cups sliced fresh shiitake mushrooms for 1½ cups of the fresh mushrooms.*

Rinse and cook rice according to package directions; set aside.

Cut enough bread into ½-inch cubes to measure 4 cups. Spread in single layer on baking sheet. Broil 5 to 6 inches from heat 4 minutes or until lightly toasted, stirring after 2 minutes; set aside.

Melt butter in large skillet over medium heat. Add onion and garlic. Cook and stir 3 minutes. Add mushrooms; cook 3 minutes, stirring occasionally. Add sage, dried thyme leaves, salt and pepper. Add cooked rice; cook 2 minutes, stirring occasionally. Stir in broth. Add pecans and toasted bread cubes; toss lightly.

Transfer to 1½-quart casserole.** Preheat oven to 325°F. Cover casserole with lid or foil. Bake 40 minutes or until heated through. Garnish, if desired.

Makes 6 to 8 servings

***At this point, Wild Rice Mushroom Stuffing may be covered and refrigerated up to 8 hours before baking. Bake 50 minutes or until heated through.*

Wild Rice Mushroom Stuffing

Sesame Green Beans and Red Pepper

1 tablespoon sesame seeds
3 tablespoons *Frank's® RedHot®* Cayenne Pepper Sauce
1 tablespoon olive oil
1 tablespoon soy sauce
2 teaspoons grated peeled fresh ginger
¼ teaspoon Oriental sesame oil
1 clove garlic, minced
1 pound fresh green beans, washed, trimmed and cut in half crosswise
¼ teaspoon salt
½ red bell pepper, seeded and cut into very thin strips
Lettuce (optional)

1. Heat large nonstick skillet over medium heat. Add sesame seeds. Cook 1 to 2 minutes or until golden; shaking skillet often. Transfer to small bowl. Whisk in ***Frank's RedHot*** Sauce, olive oil, soy sauce, ginger, sesame oil and garlic; set aside.

2. Bring 1 cup water to a boil in large saucepan over high heat. Place green beans and salt in steamer basket; set into saucepan. Do not let water touch beans. Cover; steam 5 to 6 minutes or until beans are crisp-tender. Rinse with cold water; drain well.

3. Combine beans and bell pepper in large bowl. Pour sesame dressing over vegetables; toss to coat evenly. Cover; refrigerate 1 hour. Toss just before serving. Serve on lettuce-lined plate, if desired.

Makes 6 servings

Potatoes au Gratin

1½ pounds small red potatoes
6 tablespoons margarine or butter, divided
3 tablespoons all-purpose flour
½ teaspoon salt
¼ teaspoon white pepper
1½ cups milk
1 cup (4 ounces) shredded Cheddar cheese
4 green onions, thinly sliced
¾ cup cracker crumbs

Preheat oven to 350°F. Spray 1-quart round casserole with nonstick cooking spray.

Place potatoes in 2-quart saucepan; add enough water to cover potatoes. Bring to a boil over high heat. Cook, uncovered, about 10 minutes or until partially done. Potatoes should still be firm in center. Drain and rinse in cold water until potatoes are cool. Drain and set aside.

Meanwhile, melt 4 tablespoons margarine in medium saucepan over medium heat. Add flour, salt and pepper, stirring until smooth. Gradually add milk, stirring constantly until sauce is thickened. Add cheese, stirring until melted.

Cut potatoes crosswise into ¼-inch-thick slices. Layer ⅓ of potatoes in prepared dish. Top with ⅓ of onions and ⅓ of cheese sauce. Repeat layers twice, ending with cheese sauce.

Melt remaining 2 tablespoons margarine. Combine cracker crumbs and margarine in small bowl. Sprinkle evenly over top of casserole.

Bake, uncovered, 35 to 40 minutes or until hot and bubbly and potatoes are tender.

Makes 4 to 6 servings

Orange-Glazed Carrots

- 1 pound fresh or thawed frozen baby carrots
- ⅓ cup orange marmalade
- 2 tablespoons butter
- 2 teaspoons Dijon mustard
- ½ teaspoon grated fresh ginger

Heat 1 inch lightly salted water in 2-quart saucepan over high heat to a boil; add carrots. Return to a boil. Reduce heat to low. Cover and simmer 10 to 12 minutes for fresh carrots (8 to 10 minutes for frozen carrots) or until crisp-tender. Drain well; return carrots to pan. Stir in marmalade, butter, mustard and ginger. Simmer, uncovered, over medium heat 3 minutes or until carrots are glazed, stirring occasionally.*

Makes 6 servings

**At this point, carrots may be transferred to a microwavable casserole dish with lid. Cover and refrigerate up to 8 hours before serving. To reheat, microwave at HIGH 4 to 5 minutes or until hot.*

Note: Recipe may be doubled.

Wild Rice Apple Side Dish

- 1 cup uncooked wild rice
- 3½ cups chicken broth
- ½ teaspoon ground nutmeg
- 1 cup dried apple slices
- 1 cup chopped onion
- 1 jar (4.5 ounces) sliced mushrooms, drained
- ½ cup thinly sliced celery

In large saucepan, simmer wild rice, broth and nutmeg 20 minutes. Add remaining ingredients; cover and simmer 20 to 30 minutes, stirring occasionally, until wild rice reaches desired doneness.

Makes 6 servings

Favorite recipe from Minnesota Cultivated Wild Rice Council

Sausage-Cornbread Stuffing

8 ounces bulk pork sausage (regular or spicy)
½ cup butter or margarine
2 medium onions, chopped
2 cloves garlic, minced
2 teaspoons dried sage
1 teaspoon poultry seasoning
1 package (16 ounces) prepared dry cornbread crumbs
¾ to 1¼ cups chicken broth
Sage leaves for garnish

Brown sausage in large skillet over medium-high heat until no longer pink, stirring to separate meat. Drain sausage on paper towels; set aside. Wipe skillet with paper towels to remove grease. Melt butter in same skillet over medium heat until foamy. Cook and stir onions and garlic in butter 10 minutes or until onions are softened. Stir in dried sage and poultry seasoning; cook 1 minute more.

Combine cornbread crumbs, sausage and onion mixture in large bowl. *If stuffing is to be cooked in turkey,* drizzle ¾ cup broth over stuffing; toss lightly until evenly moistened. Stuff body and neck cavities loosely with stuffing. Stuffing may be prepared up to 1 day before using. *Do not stuff turkey until just before ready to roast.* Roast according to package directions. *If stuffing is to be cooked separately,* drizzle 1¼ cups broth over stuffing; toss stuffing lightly until evenly moistened. Transfer to 3-quart casserole.

Preheat oven to 350°F. Bake 45 minutes (55 to 60 minutes if refrigerated) or until heated through. For drier stuffing, uncover during last 15 minutes of baking. Garnish, if desired.

Makes 12 cups stuffing

Harvest Casserole

1 pound maple-flavored or regular pork sausage
2 (2-pound) acorn squash
1 cup cooked rice
½ cup dried cranberries
½ teaspoon ground cinnamon
½ teaspoon salt
½ teaspoon pepper
1 can (10¾ ounces) chicken broth, divided

1. Preheat oven to 350°F.

2. Crumble sausage into skillet and cook until brown. Remove from heat and drain fat.

3. Meanwhile pierce squash in several places using sharp knife. Microwave on HIGH 8 minutes, turning over halfway through. Remove. When cool enough to handle, cut off top and bottom ½ inch of both squash. Cut squash horizontally to yield two rings each, about 1½ to 2 inches thick. Remove seeds and membrane. Place rings in a greased 11×7-inch casserole.

4. Add rice, cranberries, cinnamon, salt and pepper to sausage. Add ¼ cup chicken broth to sausage to moisten. Spoon sausage mixture into squash rings. Pour remaining broth into casserole around rings.

5. Cover dish with foil. Bake for 15 minutes. Remove foil and bake another 5 to 10 minutes, or until squash is tender.

Makes 4 servings

Note: For a side-dish casserole eliminate pork sausage and double the rice.

Harvest Casserole

Potato Pancakes with Apple-Cherry Chutney

Apple-Cherry Chutney (recipe follows)
1 pound baking potatoes (about 2 medium)
½ small onion
3 egg whites
2 tablespoons all-purpose flour
½ teaspoon salt
¼ teaspoon black pepper
4 teaspoons vegetable oil, divided

1. Prepare Apple-Cherry Chutney; set aside.

2. Wash and scrub potatoes; cut into chunks. Combine potatoes, onion, egg whites, flour, salt and pepper in food processor or blender; process until almost smooth (mixture will appear grainy).

3. Heat large nonstick skillet 1 minute over medium heat. Add 1 teaspoon oil. Spoon ⅓ cup batter per pancake into skillet. Cook 3 pancakes at a time, 3 minutes per side or until golden brown. Repeat with remaining batter, adding 1 teaspoon oil with each batch. Serve with Apple-Cherry Chutney.

Makes 6 servings (2 pancakes each)

Apple-Cherry Chutney

1 cup chunky applesauce
½ cup canned tart cherries, drained
2 tablespoons brown sugar
1 teaspoon lemon juice
½ teaspoon ground cinnamon
⅛ teaspoon nutmeg

Combine all ingredients in small saucepan; bring to a boil. Reduce heat; simmer 5 minutes. Serve warm.

Makes 1½ cups

Asparagus Wreath

1 pound fresh asparagus, ends trimmed
1 tablespoon butter or margarine
1 teaspoon lemon juice
6 thin slices pepperoni, finely chopped
¼ cup seasoned dry bread crumbs
Pimiento strips for garnish

1. Peel asparagus stalks, if desired. Steam asparagus in large covered saucepan 5 to 8 minutes or until crisp-tender.

2. Arrange asparagus in wreath shape on warm, round serving platter.

3. Heat butter and lemon juice in small saucepan until butter is melted; pour over asparagus. Combine chopped pepperoni and bread crumbs in small bowl; sprinkle over asparagus. Garnish, if desired. *Makes 4 side-dish servings*

Carrots with Raisin Sauce

2 bags (16 ounces each) BIRDS EYE® frozen Sliced Carrots
¼ cup brown sugar
1 tablespoon cornstarch
⅔ cup water
½ cup raisins
2 teaspoons cider vinegar

- Cook carrots according to package directions; drain.
- Blend brown sugar and cornstarch in small saucepan.
- Add remaining ingredients; cook over low heat until sauce is thickened and raisins are plump.
- Toss carrots with sauce. *Makes about 8 servings*

Prep Time: 2 to 3 minutes
Cook Time: 8 to 10 minutes

Spinach Spoonbread

1 package (10 ounces) frozen chopped spinach, thawed and squeezed dry
1 red bell pepper, seeded and diced
4 eggs, lightly beaten
1 cup cottage cheese
1 package (5½ ounces) cornbread mix
6 green onions, sliced
½ cup butter, melted
1¼ teaspoons seasoned salt

Slow Cooker Directions

1. Combine all ingredients in large bowl; mix well.

2. Pour batter into oiled, preheated slow cooker. Cook, covered, with lid slightly ajar to allow excess moisture to escape, on HIGH 1¾ to 2 hours or on LOW 3 to 4 hours or until edges are golden and knife inserted in center of bread comes out clean.

3. Serve bread spooned from slow cooker, or loosen edges and bottom with knife and invert onto plate. Cut into wedges to serve. *Makes 8 servings*

Cheddary Garlic Mashed Potatoes

4 cups hot mashed potatoes
1 can (10¾ ounces) condensed cream of chicken soup
1½ cups shredded Cheddar cheese, divided
⅛ teaspoon garlic powder
1½ cups *French's*® French Fried Onions

1. Preheat oven to 375°F. Heat mashed potatoes, soup, 1 cup cheese and garlic powder in saucepan over medium heat. Stir until cheese melts.

2. Spoon potato mixture into 2-quart baking dish. Top with remaining ½ cup cheese and French Fried Onions.

3. Bake 5 to 10 minutes or until hot and onions are golden. *Makes 6 to 8 servings*

Prep Time: 10 minutes
Cook Time: 5 minutes

Marinated Mushrooms, Carrots and Snow Peas

1 cup julienne carrots
1 cup fresh snow peas or sugar snap peas
½ cup water
1 lemon
2 cups small mushrooms
⅔ cup white wine vinegar
2 tablespoons sugar
2 tablespoons extra-light olive oil
1 clove garlic, minced
2 tablespoons chopped fresh parsley
1 tablespoon chopped fresh thyme

1. Combine carrots and peas in 1-quart microwavable dish; add water. Cover and microwave at HIGH 4 minutes or just until water boils. Do not drain.

2. Remove several strips of peel from lemon with vegetable peeler. Chop peel to measure 1 teaspoon. Squeeze juice from lemon to measure 2 tablespoons. Combine peel, juice and remaining ingredients in small bowl. Pour over carrot mixture. Cover and refrigerate at least 3 hours.

3. To serve, remove vegetables from marinade with slotted spoon. Place in serving dish; discard marinade.

Makes 12 servings

Roasted Potatoes and Pearl Onions

3 pounds red potatoes, well-scrubbed and cut into 1½-inch cubes
1 package (10 ounces) pearl onions, peeled
2 tablespoons olive oil
2 teaspoons dried basil leaves or thyme leaves
1 teaspoon paprika
¾ teaspoon salt
¾ teaspoon dried rosemary
¾ teaspoon black pepper

1. Preheat oven to 400°F. Spray large shallow roasting pan (do not use glass or potatoes will not brown) with nonstick cooking spray.

2. Add potatoes and onions to pan; drizzle with oil. Combine basil, paprika, salt, rosemary and pepper in small bowl; mix well. Sprinkle over potatoes and onions; toss well to coat lightly with oil and seasonings.

3. Bake 20 minutes; toss well. Continue baking 15 to 20 minutes or until potatoes are browned and tender. *Makes 8 servings*

Sherried Mushrooms

½ cup butter
1 cup HOLLAND HOUSE® Sherry Cooking Wine
1 clove garlic, crushed
18 fresh mushrooms, sliced
Salt and black pepper

Melt butter in medium skillet over medium heat. Add cooking wine and garlic. Add mushrooms; cook until tender, about 5 minutes, stirring frequently. Season to taste with salt and pepper. *Makes 2 to 3 servings*

Country Green Beans with Ham

2 teaspoons olive oil
¼ cup minced onion
1 clove garlic, minced
1 pound fresh green beans, rinsed and drained
1 cup chopped fresh tomatoes
6 slices (2 ounces) thinly sliced low-fat smoked turkey-ham
1 tablespoon chopped fresh marjoram
2 teaspoons chopped fresh basil
⅛ teaspoon black pepper
¼ cup herbed croutons

1. Heat oil in medium saucepan over medium heat. Add onion and garlic; cook and stir about 3 minutes or until onion is tender. Reduce heat to low.

2. Add green beans, tomatoes, turkey-ham, marjoram, basil and black pepper. Cook about 10 minutes, stirring occasionally, until liquid from tomatoes is absorbed.

3. Transfer mixture to serving dish. Top with croutons. *Makes 4 servings*

Carrots Amandine

1 pound carrots, peeled and cut into ½-inch diagonal slices
¼ cup golden raisins (optional)
¼ cup I CAN'T BELIEVE IT'S NOT BUTTER!® Spread
3 tablespoons honey
1 teaspoon lemon juice
¼ teaspoon ground ginger (optional)
¼ cup sliced almonds, toasted

On stovetop or in microwave oven, steam carrots and raisins until tender; drain. Stir in I Can't Believe It's Not Butter! Spread, honey, lemon juice and ginger. Spoon into serving bowl and sprinkle with almonds. *Makes 4 servings*

Old-Fashioned Herb Stuffing

6 pieces (8 ounces) whole wheat, rye or white bread (or combination), cut into ½-inch cubes
1 tablespoon margarine or butter
1 cup chopped onion
½ cup thinly sliced celery
½ cup thinly sliced carrot
1 cup canned fat-free reduced-sodium chicken broth
1 tablespoon chopped fresh thyme *or* 1 teaspoon dried thyme
1 tablespoon chopped fresh sage *or* 1 teaspoon dried sage
½ teaspoon paprika
¼ teaspoon black pepper

1. Preheat oven to 350°F. Place bread cubes on baking sheet; bake 10 minutes or until dry.

2. Melt margarine in large saucepan over medium heat. Add onion, celery and carrot; cover and cook 10 minutes or until vegetables are tender. Add broth, thyme, sage, paprika and pepper; bring to a simmer. Stir in bread pieces; mix well. Remove pan from heat; set aside.

3. Coat 1½ quart baking dish with nonstick cooking spray. Spoon stuffing into dish. Cover and bake 25 to 30 minutes or until heated through. *Makes 4 servings*

Fresh Vegetable Casserole

8 small new potatoes
8 baby carrots
1 small cauliflower, broken into florets
4 stalks asparagus, cut into 1-inch pieces
3 tablespoons butter or margarine
3 tablespoons all-purpose flour
2 cups milk
Salt
Black pepper
¾ cup (3 ounces) shredded Cheddar cheese
Chopped fresh cilantro

Cook vegetables until crisp-tender. Arrange vegetables in buttered 2-quart casserole. Preheat oven to 350°F.

To make sauce, melt butter in medium saucepan over medium heat. Stir in flour until smooth. Gradually stir in milk. Cook until thickened, stirring constantly. Season to taste with salt and pepper. Add cheese, stirring until cheese is melted. Pour sauce over vegetables and sprinkle with cilantro. Bake 15 minutes or until heated through.

Makes 4 to 6 servings

Fresh Vegetable Casserole

Honey Mustard-Orange Roasted Vegetables

6 cups assorted cut-up vegetables (red or green bell peppers, zucchini, red onions and carrots)
2 tablespoons olive oil
1 teaspoon minced garlic
¼ cup *French's*® Sweet & Tangy Honey Mustard
2 tablespoons orange juice
1 teaspoon grated orange peel

1. Preheat oven to 450°F. Toss vegetables with oil, garlic and *1 teaspoon salt* in roasting pan.

2. Bake, uncovered, 20 minutes or until tender.

3. Toss vegetables with mustard, juice and orange peel just before serving. Serve over pasta or with bread, if desired. *Makes 6 servings*

Prep Time: 10 minutes
Cook Time: 20 minutes

Orange-Spiked Zucchini and Carrots

1 pound zucchini, cut into ¼-inch slices
1 package (10 ounces) frozen sliced carrots, thawed
1 cup unsweetened orange juice
1 rib celery, finely chopped
2 tablespoons chopped onion
Salt and black pepper (optional)

Combine all ingredients in large nonstick saucepan. Simmer, covered, 10 to 12 minutes or until zucchini is tender. Uncover and continue to simmer, stirring occasionally, until most of the liquid has evaporated. *Makes 7 servings*

Beef Tenderloin with Roasted Vegetables

1 beef tenderloin (3 pounds), well trimmed
½ cup chardonnay or other dry white wine
½ cup reduced-sodium soy sauce
2 cloves garlic, sliced
1 tablespoon fresh rosemary
1 tablespoon Dijon mustard
1 teaspoon dry mustard
1 pound small red or white potatoes, cut into 1-inch pieces
1 pound brussels sprouts
12 ounces baby carrots

1. Place tenderloin in resealable plastic food storage bag. Combine wine, soy sauce, garlic, rosemary, Dijon mustard and dry mustard in small bowl. Pour over tenderloin. Seal bag; turn bag to coat. Marinate in refrigerator 4 to 12 hours, turning several times.

2. Preheat oven to 425°F. Spray 13×9-inch baking pan with nonstick cooking spray. Place potatoes, brussels sprouts and carrots in pan. Remove tenderloin from marinade. Pour marinade over vegetables; toss to coat well. Cover vegetables with foil. Bake 30 minutes; stir. Place tenderloin on vegetables. Bake 45 minutes for medium or until internal temperature reaches 145°F when tested with meat thermometer inserted into the thickest part of roast. Transfer roast to cutting board; cover with foil. Let stand 10 to 15 minutes before carving. Internal temperature will continue to rise 5°F to 10°F during stand time.

3. Stir vegetables; test for doneness and continue to bake if not tender. Slice tenderloin; arrange on serving platter with roasted vegetables. Garnish with fresh rosemary, if desired.

Makes 10 servings

Browned Pork Chops with Gravy

4 boneless pork loin chops (12 ounces)
½ teaspoon dried sage leaves
½ teaspoon dried marjoram leaves
¼ teaspoon black pepper
⅛ teaspoon salt
Nonstick olive oil cooking spray
¼ cup coarsely chopped onion
1 clove garlic, minced
1 cup sliced mushrooms
¾ cup beef broth
⅓ cup nonfat sour cream
1 tablespoon all-purpose flour
1 teaspoon Dijon mustard
2 cups hot cooked noodles
Snipped parsley (optional)

1. Trim fat from chops. Stir together sage, marjoram, pepper and salt. Rub on both sides of chops. Spray large nonstick skillet with cooking spray; heat over medium heat. Place chops in skillet. Cook 5 minutes, turning once, or until chops are just barely pink. Remove chops from skillet; keep warm.

2. Add onion and garlic to skillet; cook and stir 2 minutes. Add mushrooms and broth. Bring to a boil. Reduce heat and simmer, covered, 3 to 4 minutes or until mushrooms are tender.

3. Whisk together sour cream, flour and mustard in medium bowl. Whisk in about 3 tablespoons broth from skillet. Stir sour cream mixture into skillet. Cook, stirring constantly, until mixture comes to a boil. Serve over pork chops and noodles. Sprinkle with parsley, if desired.

Makes 4 servings

Mustard Crusted Rib Roast

1 (3-rib) standing beef rib roast, trimmed* (6 to 7 pounds)
3 tablespoons Dijon mustard
1 tablespoon plus 1½ teaspoons chopped fresh tarragon *or* 1½ teaspoons dried tarragon leaves
3 cloves garlic, minced
¼ cup dry red wine
⅓ cup finely chopped shallots (about 2 shallots)
1 tablespoon all-purpose flour
1 cup beef broth
Mashed potatoes (optional)
Fresh tarragon sprigs for garnish

**Ask meat retailer to remove chine bone for easier carving. Trim fat to ¼-inch thickness.*

1. Preheat oven to 450°F. Place roast, bone-side-down, in shallow roasting pan. Combine mustard, chopped tarragon and garlic in small bowl; spread over all surfaces of roast, except bottom. Insert meat thermometer into thickest part of roast, not touching bone or fat. Roast 10 minutes.

2. *Reduce oven temperature to 325°F.* Roast about 20 minutes per pound for medium or until internal temperature reaches 145°F on meat thermometer.

3. Transfer roast to cutting board; cover with foil. Let stand 10 to 15 minutes before carving. Internal temperature will continue to rise 5°F to 10°F during stand time.

4. To make gravy, pour fat from roasting pan, reserving 1 tablespoon in medium saucepan. Add wine to roasting pan; place over 2 burners. Cook over medium heat 2 minutes or until slightly thickened, stirring to scrape up browned bits; reserve.

5. Add shallots to reserved drippings in saucepan; cook and stir over medium heat 4 minutes or until softened. Add flour; cook and stir 1 minute. Add broth and reserved wine mixture; cook 5 minutes or until sauce thickens, stirring occasionally. Pour through strainer into gravy boat, pressing with back of spoon on shallots; discard solids.

6. Carve roast into ½-inch-thick slices. Serve with mashed potatoes and gravy. Garnish, if desired.

Makes 6 to 8 servings

Herb-Roasted Racks of Lamb

½ cup mango chutney, chopped
2 to 3 cloves garlic, minced
2 whole racks (6 ribs each) lamb loin chops (2½ to 3 pounds)
1 cup fresh French or Italian bread crumbs
1 tablespoon chopped fresh thyme *or* 1 teaspoon dried thyme leaves
1 tablespoon chopped fresh rosemary *or* 1 teaspoon dried rosemary
1 tablespoon chopped fresh oregano *or* 1 teaspoon dried oregano

1. Preheat oven to 400°F. Combine chutney and garlic in small bowl; spread evenly over meaty side of lamb with thin spatula. Combine remaining ingredients in separate small bowl; pat crumb mixture evenly over chutney mixture.

2. Place lamb racks, crumb sides up, on rack in shallow roasting pan. Roast in oven 30 to 35 minutes for medium or until internal temperature reaches 145°F when tested with meat thermometer inserted into the thickest part of lamb not touching bone.

3. Place lamb on cutting board; let stand 10 to 15 minutes before carving. Internal temperature will continue to rise 5°F to 10°F during stand time. Slice between ribs into individual chops with large carving knife. Garnish with additional fresh herbs and mango slices, if desired. Serve immediately. *Makes 4 servings*

Dad's Dill Beef Roast

1 (3- to 4-pound) beef roast
1 large jar whole dill pickles, undrained

Slow Cooker Directions
Place beef in slow cooker. Pour pickles with juice over top of beef. Cover and cook on LOW 8 to 10 hours. Shred beef with two forks.

Serving Suggestion: Pile this beef onto a toasted roll or bun, and you'll have an out-of-this world sandwich! Or, for an easy dinner variation, serve it with mashed potatoes.

Prep Time: 5 minutes

Peppered Steak with Dijon Sauce

4 boneless beef top loin or New York strip steaks, cut 1 inch thick (about 1½ pounds)
1 tablespoon *French's*® Worcestershire Sauce
Crushed black pepper
⅓ cup mayonnaise
⅓ cup *French's*® Napa Valley Style Dijon Mustard
3 tablespoons dry red wine
2 tablespoons minced red or green onion
2 tablespoons minced fresh parsley
1 clove garlic, minced

1. Brush steaks with Worcestershire and sprinkle with pepper to taste; set aside. To prepare Dijon sauce, combine mayonnaise, mustard, wine, onion, parsley and garlic in medium bowl.

2. Place steaks on grid. Grill steaks over high heat 15 minutes for medium rare or to desired doneness, turning often. Serve with Dijon sauce. Garnish as desired.

Makes 4 servings

Tip: Dijon sauce is also great served with grilled salmon and swordfish. To serve with fish, substitute white wine for red wine and minced dill for fresh parsley.

Prep Time: 10 minutes
Cook Time: 15 minutes

Smothered Steak

1½ to 2 pounds cube steak, cut into 4 pieces
All-purpose flour
1 can (10¾ ounces) condensed cream of mushroom soup, undiluted
1 can (4 ounces) sliced mushrooms
1 envelope (1 ounce) dried onion soup mix

Slow Cooker Directions
Dust steak lightly with flour. Place in slow cooker. Combine mushroom soup, mushrooms and onion soup mix in medium bowl; pour over steak. Cover and cook on LOW 6 to 8 hours.

Makes 4 servings

Glazed Roast Pork Loin with Cranberry Stuffing

1¼ cups chopped fresh or partially thawed frozen cranberries
2 teaspoons sugar
½ cup butter or margarine
1 cup chopped onion
1 package (8 ounces) herb-seasoned stuffing mix
1 cup chicken broth
½ cup peeled and diced orange
1 egg, beaten
½ teaspoon grated orange peel
1 (2½- to 3-pound) boneless center cut loin pork roast
¼ cup currant jelly
1 tablespoon cranberry liqueur or cassis

Toss cranberries with sugar in small bowl; set aside. Melt butter in saucepan over medium heat until foamy. Add onion; cook and stir until tender. Remove from heat. Combine stuffing mix, broth, orange, egg and orange peel. Add cranberry mixture and onion; toss lightly.

Preheat oven to 325°F. To butterfly roast, cut lengthwise down roast almost to, but not through bottom. Open like a book. Cover roast with plastic wrap; pound with flat side of meat mallet. Remove plastic wrap; spread roast with part of stuffing. Close halves together and tie roast with cotton string at 2-inch intervals. Place leftover stuffing in covered casserole; bake with roast during last 45 minutes of cooking time. Place roast on meat rack in foil-lined roasting pan. Insert meat thermometer into pork.

Combine jelly and liqueur. Brush half of mixture over roast after first 45 minutes in oven. Roast 30 minutes more or until internal temperature reaches 165°F when tested with meat thermometer inserted into thickest part of roast. Brush with remaining jelly mixture. Transfer roast to cutting board; cover with foil. Let stand 10 to 15 minutes before carving. Internal temperature will continue to rise 5°F to 10°F during stand time. Carve roast crosswise; serve with stuffing.

Makes 8 to 10 servings

Roasted Herb & Garlic Tenderloin

1 beef tenderloin roast, trimmed (3 to 4 pounds)
1 tablespoon black peppercorns
2 tablespoons chopped fresh basil *or* 2 teaspoons dried basil leaves
4½ teaspoons chopped fresh thyme *or* 1½ teaspoons dried thyme leaves
1 tablespoon chopped fresh rosemary *or* 1 teaspoon dried rosemary
1 tablespoon minced garlic
Salt and black pepper (optional)

1. Preheat oven to 425°F. To hold shape of roast, tie roast with cotton string at 1½-inch intervals. Place roast on meat rack in shallow roasting pan.

2. Place peppercorns in small heavy resealable plastic food storage bag. Squeeze out excess air; seal bag tightly. Pound peppercorns with flat side of meat mallet or rolling pin until peppercorns are cracked.

3. Combine cracked peppercorns, basil, thyme, rosemary and garlic in small bowl; rub over top surface of roast.

4. Roast 40 to 50 minutes until internal temperatures reaches 135°F for medium rare or 150°F for medium when tested with meat thermometer inserted into thickest part of roast.

5. Transfer roast to cutting board; cover with foil. Let stand 10 to 15 minutes before carving. Internal temperature will continue to rise 5 to 10°F during stand time. Remove and discard string. To serve, carve crosswise into ½-inch-thick slices with large carving knife. Season with salt and pepper, if desired. *Makes 10 to 12 servings*

Lamb Chops with Cranberry-Pear Chutney

Chutney

- **½ cup water**
- **¼ cup dried cranberries**
- **¼ cup dried apricots, cut into quarters**
- **¼ cup no-sugar-added raspberry spread**
- **1 tablespoon red wine vinegar**
- **¼ teaspoon cinnamon**
- **⅛ teaspoon salt**
- **1 (6-ounce) pear, peeled and cut into ½-inch pieces**
- **½ teaspoon vanilla**

Lamb

- **1¼ pounds bone-in lamb loin chops**
- **2 cloves garlic, minced**
- **¼ teaspoon dried rosemary**
- **¼ teaspoon salt**
- **Black pepper**

Preheat broiler. For chutney, combine water, cranberries, apricots, raspberry spread, vinegar, cinnamon and salt in small saucepan. Bring to boil over high heat. Reduce heat to medium-low; simmer, uncovered, 12 minutes or until mixture has thickened. Remove from heat; stir in pear and vanilla.

For lamb, rub both sides of chops with garlic. Sprinkle with rosemary, salt and pepper. Coat broiler pan and rack with nonstick cooking spray. Place lamb on rack and broil at least 5 inches from heat source 7 minutes; turn and broil 7 minutes longer or until desired doneness. Serve with chutney. *Makes 4 servings*

Swiss Steak

1 (2-pound) round steak, cut to fit into slow cooker
All-purpose flour
Salt
Black pepper
1 onion, sliced into thick rings
1 clove garlic, minced
1 can (28 ounces) whole tomatoes, undrained
1 can (10¾ ounces) condensed tomato soup, undiluted
3 medium potatoes, unpeeled, diced
1 package (16 ounces) frozen peas and carrots
1 cup sliced celery
Additional vegetables

Slow Cooker Directions

1. Dredge steak in flour seasoned with salt and pepper. Shake off excess flour.

2. Place onion and garlic in bottom of slow cooker. Add steak and tomatoes. Cover with tomato soup. Add potatoes, peas and carrots, celery and any additional vegetables. Cover and cook on HIGH 4 to 6 hours or until meat and potatoes are tender. *Makes 8 servings*

Serving Suggestion: Add corn or green beans for a very easy variation of this fabulous dish.

Prime Ribs of Beef à la Lawry's®

1 (8-pound) prime rib roast
LAWRY'S® Seasoned Salt
Rock Salt

Preheat oven to 500°F.

Score fat on meat and rub generously with Seasoned Salt. Cover bottom of roasting pan with rock salt 1 inch deep. Place roast directly on rock salt and bake, uncovered, 8 minutes per pound for rare. *Makes 8 servings*

Serving Suggestion: Garnish with watercress and spiced crab apples. Carve at tableside. Serve with additional Seasoned Salt.

Pork Roast with Dried Cranberries and Apricots

1 center cut pork loin roast (3½ pounds)
1½ cups cranberry apple juice, divided
1 cup chardonnay or other dry white wine
1½ teaspoons ground ginger
1 teaspoon ground cardamom
2 tablespoons apricot preserves
¼ cup water
1 tablespoon plus 1 teaspoon cornstarch
½ cup dried cranberries
½ cup chopped dried apricots
2 tablespoons golden raisins

1. Place pork roast in resealable plastic food storage bag. Combine 1 cup cranberry apple juice, chardonnay, ginger and cardamom in medium bowl. Pour over roast, turning to coat. Seal bag. Marinate in refrigerator 4 hours or overnight, turning several times.

2. Preheat oven to 350°F. Remove roast from marinade; reserve marinade. Place roast in roasting pan. Pour marinade over roast. Bake, loosely covered with foil, 1 hour. Remove foil and continue baking 30 minutes or until internal temperature reaches 165°F when tested with a meat thermometer inserted into the thickest part of roast. Transfer roast to cutting board; cover with foil. Internal temperature will continue to rise 5°F to 10°F during stand time.

3. Measure juices from pan. Add enough remaining cranberry apple juice to equal 1½ cups. Combine juices and apricot preserves in small saucepan. Stir water into cornstarch in cup until smooth; stir into juice mixture. Bring to a boil over medium heat. Cook until thickened, stirring frequently. Add dried cranberries, apricots and raisins. Cook 2 minutes; remove from heat. Cut roast into thin slices. Drizzle some sauce over roast; serve with remaining sauce. Garnish, if desired.

Makes 10 servings

Pork Roast with Dried Cranberries and Apricots

Pot Roast Carbonnade

6 thick slices applewood or other smoked bacon (about 6 ounces)
2 tablespoons all-purpose flour
¾ teaspoon salt
½ teaspoon black pepper
1 well-trimmed round bone* beef chuck pot roast (about 3½ pounds)
3 large Spanish onions (about 2 pounds), thinly sliced
2 tablespoons light brown sugar
1 can (about 14 ounces) beef broth
1 bottle (12 ounces) beer (not dark)
2 teaspoons dried thyme leaves, crushed
2 bay leaves
Boiled potatoes or hot cooked egg noodles (optional)
Additional black pepper (optional)
Fresh thyme sprigs for garnish

**A well-trimmed, 3-pound boneless beef chuck pot roast may be substituted; however, the bone in the pot roast will give the sauce more flavor.*

1. Preheat oven to 350°F. Cook bacon in Dutch oven over medium heat until crisp. Transfer bacon to paper towel with tongs, reserving drippings in Dutch oven. Crumble bacon; set aside.

2. Combine flour, salt and ½ teaspoon pepper in small bowl; spread on sheet of waxed paper. Place pot roast on flour mixture; roll to coat well. Place pot roast in drippings in Dutch oven. Brown over medium-low heat about 4 to 5 minutes per side, holding roast with tongs to brown all edges; remove to platter. Set aside.

3. Pour off all but 2 tablespoons drippings from dutch oven. Add onions to drippings in Dutch oven; cover and cook 10 minutes over medium heat, stirring once. Uncover; sprinkle with sugar. Cook onions, uncovered, over medium-high heat 10 minutes more or until golden brown and tender, stirring frequently.

4. Add broth, beer, thyme and bay leaves to Dutch oven; bring to a boil. Return pot roast with any accumulated juices to Dutch oven. Remove from heat; spoon sauce over top. Cover and bake 2 to 2 hours 15 minutes until meat is fork-tender.

5. Transfer meat to carving board; tent with foil.

6. Remove bay leaves; discard. Skim fat from juices with large spoon; discard. Place 1/2 of juice mixture in food processor; process until smooth. Repeat with remaining juice mixture; return puréed mixture to Dutch oven. Stir reserved bacon into sauce; cook over medium heat until heated through.

7. Discard bone from roast; carve roast into 1/4-inch-thick slices with large carving knife. Spoon sauce over roast. Serve with boiled potatoes.

8. Discard bone from roast; carve roast into 1/4-inch-thick slices with large carving knife. Spoon sauce over roast. Serve roast with boiled potatoes and additional pepper. Garnish, if desired.

Makes 8 servings

Baked Holiday Ham with Cranberry-Wine Compote

2 teaspoons peanut oil
⅔ cup chopped onion
½ cup chopped celery
1 cup red wine
1 cup honey
½ cup sugar
1 package (12 ounces) fresh cranberries
1 fully-cooked smoked ham (10 pounds)
Whole cloves
Kumquats and currant leaves for garnish

1. For Cranberry-Wine Compote, heat oil in large saucepan over medium-high heat until hot; add onion and celery. Cook until tender, stirring frequently. Stir in wine, honey and sugar; bring to a boil. Add cranberries; return to a boil. Reduce heat to low; cover and simmer 10 minutes. Cool completely.

2. Carefully ladle enough clear syrup from cranberry mixture into glass measuring cup to equal 1 cup; set aside. Transfer remaining cranberry mixture to small serving bowl; cover and refrigerate.

3. Slice away skin from ham with sharp utility knife. (Omit step if meat retailer has already removed skin.)

4. Preheat oven to 325°F. Score fat on ham in diamond design with sharp utility knife; stud with whole cloves. Place ham, fat side up, on rack in shallow roasting pan.

5. Bake, uncovered, 1½ hours. Baste ham with reserved cranberry-wine syrup. Bake 1 to 2 hours more or until meat thermometer inserted into thickest part of ham, not touching bone, registers 140°F, basting with cranberry-wine syrup twice.*

6. Let ham stand 10 minutes before transferring to warm serving platter. Slice ham with large carving knife. Serve warm with chilled Cranberry-Wine Compote. Garnish, if desired.

Makes 16 to 20 servings

**Total cooking time for ham should be 18 to 24 minutes per pound.*

Beef Stroganoff

- 8 ounces uncooked egg noodles
- ¼ cup all-purpose flour
- ½ teaspoon salt
- ¼ teaspoon black pepper
- 1¼ pounds beef tenderloin tips or tenderloin, ½ inch thick
- ¼ cup butter, divided
- ¾ cup chopped onion
- 12 ounces fresh button mushrooms, sliced
- 1 can (10½ ounces) condensed beef broth
- 2 tablespoons tomato paste
- 1 tablespoon Worcestershire sauce
- 1 cup sour cream, at room temperature
- Fresh chives for garnish

1. Cook noodles according to package directions; drain and keep warm.

2. Meanwhile, combine flour, salt and pepper in large resealable plastic food storage bag. Cut beef into 1½×½-inch strips; add ½ of beef to flour mixture. Seal bag; shake to coat well. Repeat with remaining beef.

3. Melt 1 tablespoon butter in large nonstick skillet over medium-high heat. Add ½ of beef mixture to skillet. Cook and stir until browned on all sides. *Do not overcook.* Transfer to medium bowl. Repeat with 1 tablespoon butter and remaining beef mixture; transfer to same bowl. Set aside.

4. Melt remaining 2 tablespoons butter in same skillet over medium-high heat. Add onion; cook 5 minutes, stirring occasionally. Add mushrooms; cook and stir 5 minutes or until mushrooms are tender.

5. Stir in broth, tomato paste and Worcestershire sauce; bring to a boil, scraping up any browned bits.

6. Return beef mixture and any accumulated juices to skillet; cook about 5 minutes or until heated through and sauce thickens. Stir in sour cream; heat through. *Do not boil.*

7. Serve beef mixture over reserved noodles. Garnish, if desired.

Makes 4 servings

Peppered Beef Rib Roast

1½ tablespoons black peppercorns
1 boneless beef rib roast (2½ to 3 pounds), well trimmed
¼ cup Dijon mustard
2 cloves garlic, minced
Sour Cream Sauce (recipe follows)

Prepare grill for indirect cooking.

Place peppercorns in small resealable plastic food storage bag. Squeeze out excess air; close bag securely. Pound peppercorns using flat side of meat mallet or rolling pin until cracked. Set aside.

Pat roast dry with paper towels. Combine mustard and garlic in small bowl; spread over top and sides of roast. Sprinkle pepper over mustard mixture.

Place roast, pepper-side up, on grid directly over drip pan. Grill, covered, over medium heat 1 hour to 1 hour 10 minutes for medium or until internal temperature reaches 145°F when tested with meat thermometer inserted into the thickest part of roast, adding 4 to 9 briquets to both sides of the fire after 45 minutes to maintain medium heat.

Meanwhile, prepare Sour Cream Sauce. Cover; refrigerate until serving.

Transfer roast to cutting board; cover with foil. Let stand 10 to 15 minutes before carving. Internal temperature will continue to rise 5°F to 10°F during stand time. Serve with Sour Cream Sauce.

Makes 6 to 8 servings

Sour Cream Sauce

¾ cup sour cream
2 tablespoons prepared horseradish
1 tablespoon balsamic vinegar
½ teaspoon sugar

Combine all ingredients in small bowl; mix well.

Makes about 1 cup

Peppered Beef Rib Roast

Roast Beef with Red Wine Gravy

2 tablespoons oil
1 sirloin tip roast (3 to 4 pounds)
Salt and black pepper
2 tablespoons all-purpose flour
1 jar (7 ounces) cocktail onions, drained
1 can (14½ ounces) beef broth
2 tablespoons HOLLAND HOUSE® Red Cooking Wine

Heat oven to 350°F. Heat oil in Dutch oven. Season roast to taste with salt and pepper; brown on all sides. Remove from Dutch oven. Drain excess fat, reserving ¼ cup drippings in Dutch oven. Sprinkle flour over reserved drippings. Cook over medium heat until lightly browned, stirring constantly. Add roast and onions to Dutch oven. Roast for 1¾ to 2¼ hours or until desired doneness. Remove roast to cutting board. Let stand 5 to 10 minutes before slicing. Gradually stir in beef broth and cooking wine. Bring to a boil; reduce heat. Cook until gravy thickens. Slice roast and arrange with onions on serving platter. Serve with gravy. *Makes 6 servings*

Pork Chop & Wild Rice Bake

1 package (6 ounces) seasoned long grain & wild rice mix
1⅓ cups *French's®* French Fried Onions, divided
1 package (10 ounces) frozen cut green beans, thawed and drained
¼ cup orange juice
1 teaspoon grated orange peel
4 boneless pork chops (1 inch thick)

1. Preheat oven to 375°F. Combine rice mix and seasoning packet, *2 cups water, ⅔ cup* French Fried Onions, green beans, orange juice and orange peel in 2-quart shallow baking dish. Arrange pork chops on top.

2. Bake, uncovered, 30 minutes or until pork chops are no longer pink near center. Sprinkle chops with remaining *⅔ cup* onions. Bake 5 minutes or until onions are golden. *Makes 4 servings*

Prep Time: 5 minutes
Cook Time: 35 minutes

Roast Beef with Red Wine Gravy and Sherried Mushrooms (page 134)

Veal Chops with Brandied Apricots and Pecans

8 dried apricot halves
¼ cup water
¼ cup honey
4 (¾-inch-thick) boneless veal chops (about 5 ounces each)*
¼ teaspoon salt
¼ teaspoon black pepper
3 tablespoons all-purpose flour
2 tablespoons butter or margarine
16 pecan halves
2 tablespoons brandy
Celery or mint leaves for garnish

**If boneless chops are unavailable, chops with bones may be substituted.*

1. Cut apricot halves into ¼-inch slivers.

2. Combine water and honey in 2-cup glass measuring cup; microwave at HIGH 2 minutes or until mixture begins to boil. Stir in slivered apricots; cover with plastic wrap, turning back 1 corner to vent. Microwave 30 seconds more; let stand, covered, 1 hour.

3. Meanwhile, sprinkle veal chops with salt and pepper. Place flour in shallow bowl; dredge veal chops, 1 at a time, in flour, shaking off excess.

4. Melt butter in large skillet over medium heat; arrange veal chops and pecan halves in single layer in skillet. Cook veal chops and pecans 5 minutes per side or until browned.

5. Add apricot mixture and brandy; bring to a boil. Reduce heat to low; cover and simmer 10 minutes or until veal chops are tender.

6. Transfer veal chops and pecans to 4 warm serving plates with slotted spatula. Bring apricot mixture in skillet to a boil over high heat; cook 1 minute or until slightly thickened. To serve, spoon apricot mixture over veal chops. Garnish, if desired.

Makes 4 servings

Marinated Pork Roast

½ cup GRANDMA'S® Molasses
½ cup Dijon mustard
¼ cup tarragon vinegar
Boneless pork loin roast (3 to 4 pounds)

1. In large plastic bowl, combine molasses, mustard and tarragon vinegar; mix well. Add pork to molasses mixture, turning to coat all sides. Marinate, covered, 1 to 2 hours at room temperature or overnight in refrigerator, turning several times.

2. Heat oven to 325°F. Remove pork from marinade; reserve marinade. Place pork in shallow roasting pan. Cook for 1 to 2 hours or until meat thermometer inserted into thickest part of roast reaches 160°F, basting with marinade* every 30 minutes; discard remaining marinade. Slice roast and garnish, if desired.

Makes 6 to 8 servings

**Do not baste during last 5 minutes of cooking.*

Golden Glazed Flank Steak

1 envelope LIPTON® RECIPE SECRETS® Onion Soup Mix*
1 jar (12 ounces) apricot or peach preserves
½ cup water
1 beef flank steak (about 2 pounds), cut into thin strips
2 medium green, red and/or yellow bell peppers, sliced
Hot cooked rice

**Also terrific with LIPTON® RECIPE SECRETS® Onion-Mushroom Soup Mix.*

1. In small bowl, combine soup mix, preserves and water; set aside.

2. On heavy-duty aluminum foil or in bottom of broiler pan with rack removed, arrange steak and green peppers; top with soup mixture.

3. Broil, turning steak and vegetables once, until steak is done. Serve over hot rice.

Makes 8 servings

Marinated Pork Roast with Baked Apple (page 234)

London Broil with Marinated Vegetables

¾ cup olive oil
¾ cup red wine
2 tablespoons red wine vinegar
2 tablespoons finely chopped shallots
2 teaspoons bottled minced garlic
½ teaspoon dried marjoram leaves
½ teaspoon dried oregano leaves
½ teaspoon dried basil leaves
½ teaspoon black pepper
2 pounds top round London broil (1½ inches thick)
1 medium red onion, cut into ¼-inch-thick slices
1 package (8 ounces) sliced mushrooms
1 medium red bell pepper, cut into strips
1 medium zucchini, cut into ¼-inch-thick slices

1. Combine olive oil, wine, vinegar, shallots, garlic, marjoram, oregano, basil and pepper in medium bowl; whisk to combine.

2. Combine London broil and ¾ cup marinade in large resealable food storage bag. Seal bag and turn to coat. Marinate up to 24 hours in refrigerator, turning once or twice.

3. Combine onion, mushrooms, bell pepper, zucchini and remaining marinade in separate large food storage bag. Seal bag and turn to coat. Refrigerate up to 24 hours, turning once or twice.

4. Preheat broiler. Remove meat from marinade and place on broiler pan; discard marinade. Broil 4 to 5 inches from heat about 9 minutes per side or until desired doneness. Let stand 10 minutes before slicing. Cut meat into thin slices.

5. While meat is standing, drain marinade from vegetables and arrange on broiler pan. Broil 4 to 5 inches from heat about 9 minutes or until edges of vegetables just begin to brown. Serve meat and vegetables immediately on platter.

Makes 6 servings

Make-Ahead Time: Up to 1 day before serving
Final Prep and Cook Time: 24 minutes

London Broil with Marinated Vegetables

Pork Chops and Apple Stuffing Bake

6 (¾-inch-thick) boneless pork loin chops (about 1½ pounds)
¼ teaspoon salt
⅛ teaspoon black pepper
1 tablespoon vegetable oil
1 small onion, chopped
2 ribs celery, chopped
2 Granny Smith apples, peeled, cored and coarsely chopped (about 2 cups)
1 can (14½ ounces) reduced-sodium chicken broth
1 can (10¾ ounces) condensed cream of celery soup, undiluted
¼ cup dry white wine
6 cups herb-seasoned stuffing cubes

Preheat oven to 375°F. Spray 13×9-inch baking dish with nonstick cooking spray.

Season both sides of pork chops with salt and pepper. Heat oil in large deep skillet over medium-high heat until hot. Add chops and cook until browned on both sides, turning once. Remove chops from skillet; set aside.

Add onion and celery to same skillet. Cook and stir 3 minutes or until onion is tender. Add apples; cook and stir 1 minute. Add broth, soup and wine; mix well. Bring to a simmer; remove from heat. Stir in stuffing cubes until evenly moistened.

Spread stuffing mixture evenly in prepared dish. Place pork chops on top of stuffing; pour any accumulated juices over chops.

Cover tightly with foil and bake 30 to 40 minutes or until pork chops are juicy and barely pink in center.

Makes 6 servings

Tenderloin Deluxe with Mushroom Sauce

10 tablespoons I CAN'T BELIEVE IT'S NOT BUTTER!® Spread, divided
¼ cup chopped green onions
1 tablespoon Dijon-style mustard
1 teaspoon soy sauce
2½- to 3-pound beef tenderloin
8 ounces mushrooms, sliced
2 medium onions, finely chopped
2 cloves garlic, finely chopped
⅓ cup dry sherry
4 drops hot pepper sauce
1 cup beef broth

Preheat oven to 425°F.

In small bowl, blend 4 tablespoons I Can't Believe It's Not Butter! Spread, green onions, mustard and soy sauce. In 13×9-inch baking or roasting pan, arrange beef and evenly spread with mustard mixture.

Bake, uncovered, 15 minutes. Decrease heat to 400°F. and bake 45 minutes or until desired doneness. Let stand 10 minutes before slicing.

Meanwhile, in 12-inch skillet, melt remaining 6 tablespoons I Can't Believe It's Not Butter! Spread over medium-high heat and cook mushrooms, stirring occasionally, 3 minutes or until softened. Stir in onions and cook, stirring occasionally, 12 minutes or until golden brown. Add garlic and cook 30 seconds. Stir in sherry and hot pepper sauce and cook 2 minutes. Stir in broth and simmer 5 minutes or until sauce is slightly thickened. Serve sauce over sliced beef. *Makes 6 servings*

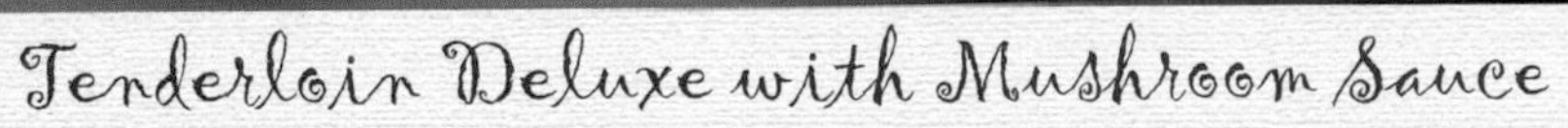

Veal Escallops with Fruited Wild Rice Stuffing

3⅓ cups cooked U.S. wild rice
1 cup chopped dried apricots
½ cup butter, softened, divided
½ cup fresh bread crumbs
½ cup chopped nuts, toasted (optional)
2 egg whites
4 tablespoons raisins
Salt and black pepper to taste
10 boned veal cutlets (3 ounces each), pounded thin
½ pound shiitake mushrooms, sliced
½ cup minced shallots
2 teaspoons minced fresh thyme
All-purpose flour
2 cups dry white wine

Mix wild rice, apricots, ¼ cup butter, bread crumbs, nuts, if desired, egg whites, raisins, salt and pepper in medium bowl. Spread approximately ½ cup mixture on each cutlet; roll each cutlet and tie with string. Set aside. Sauté mushrooms and shallots in remaining ¼ cup butter 5 minutes in large saucepan. Season with thyme, salt and pepper. Remove mushroom mixture from pan; set aside. Flour rolled cutlets; brown in same pan. Add wine and mushroom mixture; cover and braise 15 minutes over low heat. Slice and serve with mushroom sauce. *Makes 10 servings*

Favorite recipe from **California Wild Rice Advisory Board**

Spice-Rubbed Beef Brisket

2 cups hickory chips
1 teaspoon salt
1 teaspoon paprika
1 teaspoon chili powder
1 teaspoon garlic pepper
1 beef brisket (3 to 3½ pounds)
¼ cup beer or beef broth
1 tablespoon Worcestershire sauce
1 tablespoon balsamic vinegar
1 teaspoon olive oil
¼ teaspoon dry mustard
6 ears corn, cut into 2-inch pieces
12 small new potatoes
6 carrots, cut into 2-inch pieces
2 green bell peppers, cut into 2-inch squares
6 tablespoons lemon juice
1½ teaspoons salt-free dried Italian seasoning

1. Cover hickory chips with water and soak 30 minutes. Prepare grill for indirect grilling. Bank briquets on either side of water-filled drip pan.

2. Combine salt, paprika, chili powder and garlic pepper; rub spice mixture on both sides of brisket; loosely cover with foil and set aside. Combine beer, Worcestershire sauce, vinegar, oil and dry mustard.

3. Drain hickory chips and sprinkle ½ cup over coals. Place brisket directly over drip pan; grill on covered grill over medium coals 30 minutes. Baste and turn over every 30 minutes for 3 hours or until meat thermometer reaches 160°F when inserted in thickest part of brisket. Add 4 to 9 briquets and ¼ cup hickory chips to each side of fire every hour.

4. Alternately thread vegetables onto metal skewers. Combine lemon juice with 6 tablespoons water and Italian seasoning; brush on vegetables. Grill vegetables with brisket 20 to 25 minutes or until tender, turning once.

5. Remove brisket to cutting board; tent loosely with foil and let stand 10 minutes before carving. Remove excess fat. Serve with vegetable kabobs. Garnish as desired.

Makes 12 servings

Spice-Rubbed Beef Brisket
187

Pleasant Poultry

Roasted Turkey Breast with Cherry & Apple Rice Stuffing

3¾ cups water
3 boxes UNCLE BEN'S® Long Grain & Wild Rice Butter & Herb Fast Cook Recipe
½ cup butter or margarine, divided
½ cup dried red tart cherries
1 large apple, peeled and chopped (about 1 cup)
½ cup sliced almonds, toasted*
1 bone-in turkey breast (5 to 6 pounds)

**To toast almonds, place them on a baking sheet. Bake 10 to 12 minutes in preheated 325°F oven or until golden brown, stirring occasionally.*

1. In large saucepan, combine water, rice, contents of seasoning packets, 3 tablespoons butter and cherries. Bring to a boil. Cover; reduce heat to low and simmer 25 minutes or until all water is absorbed. Stir in apple and almonds; set aside.

2. Preheat oven to 325°F. Place turkey breast, skin side down, on rack in roasting pan. Loosely fill breast cavity with rice stuffing. (Place any remaining stuffing in greased baking dish; cover and refrigerate. Bake alongside turkey for 35 to 40 minutes or until heated through.)

3. Place sheet of heavy-duty foil over stuffing, molding it slightly over sides of turkey. Carefully invert turkey, skin side up, on rack. Melt remaining 5 tablespoons butter; brush some of butter over surface of turkey.

4. Roast turkey, uncovered, 1 hour; baste with melted butter. Continue roasting 1¼ to 1¾ hours, basting occasionally with melted butter, until meat thermometer inserted into center of thickest part of turkey breast, not touching bone, registers 170°F. Let turkey stand, covered, 15 minutes before carving. *Makes 6 to 8 servings*

Garlic 'n Lemon Roast Chicken

1 small onion, finely chopped
1 envelope LIPTON® RECIPE SECRETS® Savory Herb with Garlic Soup Mix
2 tablespoons olive or vegetable oil
2 tablespoons lemon juice
1 (3½-pound) roasting chicken

1. In large plastic bag or bowl, combine onion and soup mix blended with oil and lemon juice; add chicken. Close bag and shake, or toss in bowl, until chicken is evenly coated. Cover and marinate in refrigerator, turning occasionally, 2 hours.

2. Preheat oven to 350°F. Place chicken and marinade in 13×9-inch baking or roasting pan. Arrange chicken, breast side up; discard bag.

3. Bake uncovered, basting occasionally, 1 hour and 20 minutes or until meat thermometer reaches 180°F. (Insert meat thermometer into thickest part of thigh between breast and thigh; make sure tip does not touch bone.) *Makes 4 servings*

Turkey Apple Grill

1 BUTTERBALL® Fully Cooked Smoked Young Turkey, thawed, sliced thin
4 tablespoons butter or margarine
8 slices marbled rye bread
⅓ cup sour cream
⅓ cup chutney
1 tart apple, cored and sliced thin
1 cup (4 ounces) shredded Swiss cheese

Butter one side of each slice of bread. Turn buttered side down. Combine sour cream and chutney. Spread 2 tablespoons sour cream mixture on each slice of bread. Top half of the slices with turkey, apple and cheese. Top with remaining bread slices, buttered side up. Heat large skillet or griddle over medium heat until hot. Cook sandwiches about 3 minutes on each side or until golden brown and heated through. *Makes 4 sandwiches*

Prep Time: 15 minutes

Garlic 'n Lemon Roast Chicken 191

Orange-Ginger Broiled Cornish Hens

2 large Cornish hens, split (about 1½ pounds each)
2 teaspoons peanut or vegetable oil, divided
¼ cup orange marmalade
1 tablespoon minced fresh ginger

1. Place hens, skin side up, on rack of foil-lined broiler pan. Brush with 1 teaspoon oil.

2. Broil 6 to 7 inches from heat 10 minutes. Turn hens skin side down; brush with remaining 1 teaspoon oil. Broil 10 minutes.

3. Combine marmalade and ginger in cup; brush half of mixture over hens. Broil 5 minutes.

4. Turn hens skin side up; brush with remaining marmalade mixture. Broil 5 minutes or until juices run clear and hens are browned and glazed. *Makes 4 servings*

Rosemary Roasted Chicken and Potatoes

1 BUTTERBALL® Fresh Young Roaster, giblets removed
3 cloves garlic, minced
Grated peel and juice of 1 lemon
2 tablespoons vegetable oil
1 tablespoon fresh rosemary leaves
1 teaspoon cracked black pepper
¼ teaspoon salt
6 medium potatoes, cut into pieces

Preheat oven to 425°F. Mix garlic, lemon peel, lemon juice, oil, rosemary, pepper and salt in medium bowl. Place chicken, breast side up, in lightly oiled large roasting pan. Place potatoes around chicken. Drizzle garlic mixture over chicken and onto potatoes. Bake 20 to 25 minutes per pound or until internal temperature reaches 180°F in thigh. Stir potatoes occasionally to brown evenly. Let chicken stand 10 minutes before carving. *Makes 8 servings*

Prep Time: 15 minutes plus roasting time

Orange-Ginger Broiled Cornish Hen

Turkey and Stuffing Bake

- 1 jar (4½ ounces) sliced mushrooms
- ¼ cup butter or margarine
- ½ cup diced celery
- ½ cup chopped onion
- 1¼ cups HIDDEN VALLEY® The Original Ranch® Dressing, divided
- ⅔ cup water
- 3 cups seasoned stuffing mix
- ⅓ cup sweetened dried cranberries
- 3 cups coarsely shredded cooked turkey (about 1 pound)

Drain mushrooms, reserving liquid; set aside. Melt butter over medium high heat in a large skillet. Add celery and onion; sauté for 4 minutes or until soft. Remove from heat and stir in ½ cup dressing, water and reserved mushroom liquid. Stir in stuffing mix and cranberries until thoroughly moistened. Combine turkey, mushrooms and remaining ¾ cup dressing in a separate bowl; spread evenly in a greased 8-inch baking dish. Top with stuffing mixture. Bake at 350°F. for 40 minutes or until bubbly and brown.

Makes 4 to 6 servings

Festive Chicken Rolls

- 1 can (8 ounces) crushed pineapple, well drained, divided
- 2 slices cinnamon raisin bread, toasted, cubed
- ⅓ cup chopped toasted walnuts
- 4 large skinless boneless chicken breast halves
- 1 tablespoon vegetable oil
- ½ cup HEINZ® Tomato Ketchup
- ½ cup whole berry cranberry sauce
- ¼ cup orange juice
- 3 tablespoons orange marmalade
- ⅛ teaspoon ground cloves

Measure ½ cup pineapple; reserve remainder. For stuffing, combine ½ cup pineapple, toast and walnuts. Flatten chicken breasts to uniform thickness. Place about ⅓ cup stuffing across center of each breast; fold edges to center and secure with toothpicks. In skillet, brown chicken in oil on all sides. Combine ketchup with reserved pineapple and remaining ingredients; pour over chicken. Simmer, uncovered, 13 to 15 minutes, turning and basting frequently. Remove toothpicks.

Makes 4 servings

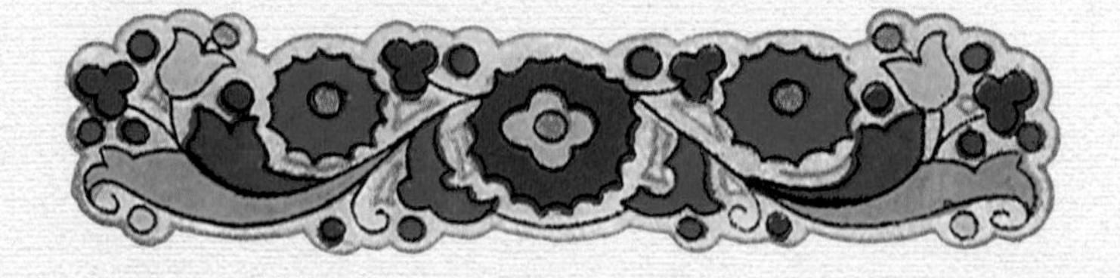

Roasted Cornish Hens with Double Mushroom Stuffing

2 Cornish hens (about 1½ pounds each)
½ teaspoon salt
¼ teaspoon ground black pepper
3 tablespoons I CAN'T BELIEVE IT'S NOT BUTTER!® Spread
1 tablespoon finely chopped shallot or onion
2 teaspoons chopped fresh tarragon leaves *or* ½ teaspoon dried tarragon leaves, crushed (optional)
½ lemon, cut in 2 wedges
Double Mushroom Stuffing (recipe page 197)
1 tablespoon all-purpose flour

Preheat oven to 425°F. Season hens and hen cavities with salt and pepper.

In small bowl, blend I Can't Believe It's Not Butter! Spread, shallot and tarragon. Evenly spread under skin, then place 1 lemon wedge in each hen.

In 18×12-inch roasting pan, on rack, arrange hens breast side up; tie legs together with string. Roast, uncovered, 15 minutes.

Meanwhile, prepare Double Mushroom Stuffing.

Decrease heat to 350°F and place Double Mushroom Stuffing casserole in oven with hens. Continue roasting hens 30 minutes or until meat thermometer inserted in thickest part of the thigh reaches 180°F and stuffing is golden. Remove hens to serving platter and keep warm. Remove rack from pan.

Skim fat from pan drippings. Blend flour with reserved broth from stuffing; stir into pan drippings. Place roasting pan over heat and bring to a boil over high heat, stirring frequently. Reduce heat to low and simmer, stirring occasionally, 1 minute or until gravy is thickened. Serve gravy and stuffing with hens. *Makes 2 servings*

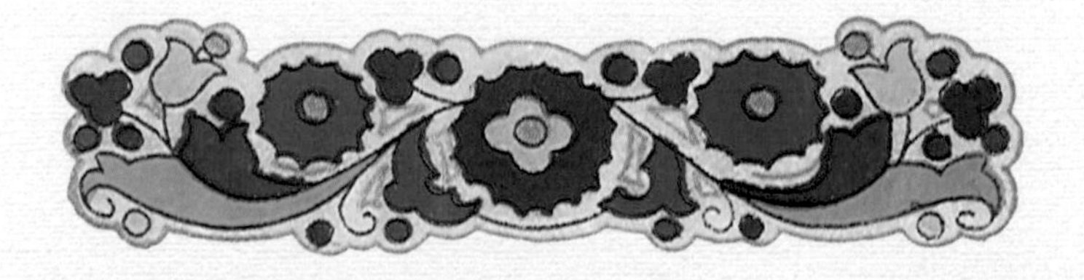

Double Mushroom Stuffing

3 tablespoons I CAN'T BELIEVE IT'S NOT BUTTER!® Spread
½ cup chopped onion
2 cups sliced white and/or shiitake mushrooms
2½ cups fresh ½-inch Italian or French bread cubes
1 can (14½ ounces) chicken broth
2 tablespoons chopped fresh parsley

In 12-inch nonstick skillet, melt I Can't Believe It's Not Butter! Spread over medium-high heat. Cook onion, stirring occasionally, 2 minutes or until softened. Add mushrooms; cook, stirring occasionally, 4 minutes or until golden. Stir in bread, ¾ cup broth (reserve remaining broth) and parsley. Season, if desired, with salt and ground black pepper. Spoon into greased 1-quart casserole. During last 30 minutes of roasting, place stuffing casserole in oven with hens. Cook until stuffing is heated through and golden. *Makes 2 servings*

Apple Pecan Chicken Roll-Ups

½ cup apple juice
½ cup UNCLE BEN'S® Instant Brown Rice
½ cup finely chopped unpeeled apple
¼ cup chopped pecans
3 tablespoons sliced green onions
4 boneless, skinless chicken breasts (about 1 pound)
1 tablespoon vegetable oil

1. Heat oven to 400°F. In small saucepan, bring apple juice to a boil. Add rice, cover, reduce heat and simmer 8 to 10 minutes or until liquid is absorbed. Stir in apple, pecans and green onions. Remove from heat.

2. Flatten each chicken breast to about ¼-inch thickness by pounding between two pieces of waxed paper. Place ¼ of rice mixture on each chicken breast. Roll up, tucking in edges. Secure with toothpicks.

3. Heat oil in medium skillet over medium-high heat. Add chicken and cook 4 to 5 minutes or until lightly browned; place in shallow baking pan. Bake 20 to 25 minutes or until chicken is no longer pink in center. *Makes 4 servings*

Cook's Tip: For this recipe, choose an apple variety that will retain its shape when cooked, such as Granny Smith, Golden Delicious or Jonathan.

Harvest Chicken

1 can (10¾ ounces) reduced-fat condensed cream of chicken soup
½ cup fat-free (skim) milk
¾ teaspoon dried Italian seasoning
¼ teaspoon dried thyme leaves
4 boneless skinless chicken breast halves
2 medium red or green apples, cored and sliced
1 small onion, thinly sliced into rings

Combine soup, milk, Italian seasoning and thyme in small bowl; set aside. Spray large nonstick skillet with nonstick cooking spray. Heat over medium heat 1 minute. Add chicken; brown 5 minutes on each side. Remove from skillet.

Add apples and onion to skillet; cook until onion is tender. Stir in soup mixture. Return chicken to skillet; reduce heat to low. Cover and simmer 5 to 10 minutes or until chicken is no longer pink in center. *Makes 4 servings*

Apple Pecan Chicken Roll-Up
199

Roast Turkey with Pan Gravy

1 fresh or thawed frozen turkey (12 to 14 pounds), reserve giblets and neck (discard liver or reserve for another use)
Sausage-Cornbread Stuffing (recipe page 123) or prepared stuffing (optional)
2 cloves garlic, minced
½ cup butter, melted
Turkey Broth with Giblets (recipe page 201)
1 cup dry white wine or vermouth
3 tablespoons all-purpose flour
Salt and black pepper

Preheat oven to 450°F. Rinse turkey; pat dry with paper towels. Prepare stuffing, if desired. Stuff body and neck cavities loosely with stuffing, if desired. Fold skin over openings and close with skewers. Tie legs together with cotton string or tuck through skin flap, if provided. Tuck wings under turkey. Place turkey on meat rack in shallow roasting pan. Stir garlic into butter. Insert meat thermometer in thickest part of thigh not touching bone. Brush 1/3 of butter mixture evenly over turkey. Place turkey in oven. *Reduce oven temperature to 325°F.* Roast 18 to 20 minutes per pound for unstuffed turkey or 22 to 24 minutes per pound for stuffed turkey, brushing with butter mixture after 1 hour and then after 1½ hours. Baste with pan juices every hour of roasting. (Total roasting time should be 4 to 5 hours.) If turkey is overbrowning, tent with foil. Cook until internal temperature reaches 180°F when tested with meat thermometer inserted into the thickest part of thigh, not touching bone.

While turkey is roasting, prepare Turkey Broth with Giblets.

Transfer turkey to cutting board; tent with foil. Let stand 15 minutes while preparing gravy. Pour off and reserve juices from roasting pan. To deglaze pan, pour wine into pan. Place over burners and cook over medium-high heat; scrape up browned bits and stir constantly 2 to 3 minutes or until mixture has reduced by about half.

Spoon off 1/3 cup fat from pan drippings; discard remaining fat.* Place 1/3 cup fat in large saucepan. Add flour; cook over medium heat 1 minute, stirring constantly.

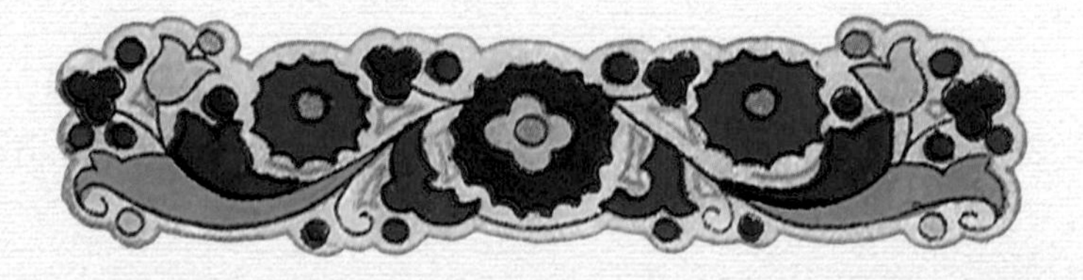

Slowly stir in 3 cups Turkey Broth, defatted turkey drippings and deglazed wine mixture from roasting pan. Cook over medium heat 10 minutes, stirring occasionally. Stir in reserved chopped giblets; heat through. Season with salt and pepper to taste.

Makes 12 servings and 3½ cups gravy

**Or, substitute ⅓ cup butter or margarine for turkey fat.*

Creamy Turkey Gravy: Stir in 1 cup heavy cream with giblets; proceed as recipe directs. Makes 4½ cups gravy.

Turkey Broth with Giblets

Reserved giblets and neck from turkey
4 cups water
1 can (13¾ ounces) chicken broth
1 medium onion, cut into quarters
2 medium carrots, coarsely chopped
4 large parsley sprigs
1 bay leaf
1 teaspoon dried thyme leaves, crushed
10 whole black peppercorns

For broth, combine giblets and neck, water and chicken broth in 3-quart saucepan. Bring to a boil over high heat; skim off foam. Stir in onion, carrots, parsley, bay leaf, thyme and peppercorns. Reduce heat to low. Simmer, uncovered, 1½ to 2 hours, stirring occasionally. (If liquid evaporates too quickly, add additional ½ cup water.) Cool to room temperature.

Strain broth; set aside. If broth measures less than 3 cups, add water to equal 3 cups liquid. If broth measures more than 3 cups, bring to a boil and heat until liquid is reduced to 3 cups. Remove meat from neck and chop giblets finely; set aside. Broth may be prepared up to 1 day before serving. Cover giblets and broth separately and refrigerate.

Makes 3 cups

Artichoke-Olive Chicken Bake

1½ cups uncooked rotini
1 tablespoon olive oil
1 medium onion, chopped
½ green bell pepper, chopped
2 cups shredded cooked chicken
1 can (14½ ounces) diced tomatoes with Italian-style herbs, undrained
1 can (14 ounces) artichoke hearts, drained and quartered
1 can (6 ounces) sliced black olives, drained
1 teaspoon dried Italian seasoning
2 cups (8 ounces) shredded mozzarella cheese

Preheat oven to 350°F. Spray 2-quart casserole with nonstick cooking spray.

Cook pasta according to package directions until al dente. Drain and set aside.

Meanwhile, heat oil in large deep skillet over medium heat until hot. Add onion and pepper; cook and stir 1 minute. Add chicken, tomatoes with juice, pasta, artichokes, olives and Italian seasoning; mix until combined.

Place half of chicken mixture in prepared dish; sprinkle with half of cheese. Top with remaining chicken mixture and cheese.

Bake, covered, 35 minutes or until hot and bubbly.

Makes 8 servings

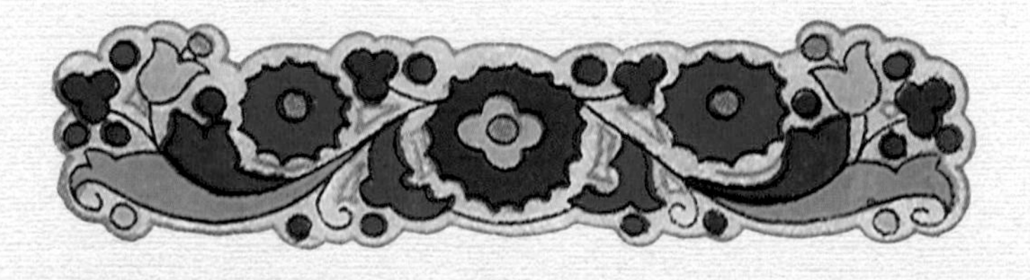

Artichoke-Olive Chicken Bake
203
CLOVES

Turkey and Biscuits

2 cans (10¾ ounces each) condensed cream of chicken soup, undiluted
¼ cup dry white wine
¼ teaspoon poultry seasoning
2 packages (8 ounces each) frozen cut asparagus, thawed
3 cups cubed cooked turkey or chicken
Paprika (optional)
1 can (11 ounces) refrigerated flaky biscuits

Preheat oven to 350°F. Spray 13×9-inch baking dish with nonstick cooking spray.

Combine soup, wine and poultry seasoning in medium bowl.

Arrange asparagus in single layer in prepared dish. Place turkey evenly over asparagus. Spread soup mixture over turkey. Sprinkle lightly with paprika, if desired.

Cover tightly with foil and bake 20 minutes. Remove from oven. *Increase oven temperature to 425°F.* Top with biscuits and bake, uncovered, 8 to 10 minutes or until biscuits are golden brown. *Makes 6 servings*

Mandarin Orange Chicken

⅓ cup HOLLAND HOUSE® White Cooking Wine
3 ounces frozen orange juice concentrate, thawed
¼ cup orange marmalade
½ teaspoon ground ginger
4 boneless chicken breast halves (about 1 pound)
1 can (11 ounces) mandarin orange segments, drained
½ cup green grapes, halved

Heat oven to 350°F. In 12×8-inch (2-quart) baking dish, combine cooking wine, concentrate, marmalade and ginger; mix well. Add chicken; turn to coat. Bake 45 to 60 minutes, or until chicken is tender and no longer pink in center, basting occasionally.* Add orange segments and grapes during last 5 minutes of cooking.
Makes 4 servings

**Do not baste during last 5 minutes of cooking.*

Swiss Melt Chicken

1 tablespoon olive oil
¼ cup minced onion
1 clove garlic, minced
4 boneless skinless chicken breasts
1 package (about 6 ounces) long grain and wild rice
1⅔ cups chicken broth
1 cup sliced mushrooms
½ cup chopped green bell pepper
½ cup chopped red bell pepper
4 slices Swiss cheese

1. Heat oil in large skillet over medium heat. Add onion and garlic; cook and stir 2 minutes or until onion is soft. Add chicken; cook 5 to 7 minutes until light brown, turning once. Add rice, contents of seasoning packet and broth. Bring to a boil. Cover; simmer 20 minutes or until rice is done.

2. Stir in mushrooms and bell peppers. Cook, covered, 5 to 8 minutes or until chicken is no longer pink in center and juices run clear when cut.

3. Place cheese over chicken; remove from heat. Let stand, covered, 5 minutes or until cheese is melted. Season to taste.

Makes 4 servings

Orange-Glazed Chicken

1 teaspoon salt
½ teaspoon black pepper
1 broiler-fryer chicken (2½ to 3 pounds), cut into halves
½ cup orange marmalade
3 tablespoons butter
1 tablespoon dried onion flakes
1 clove garlic, minced
¼ dried thyme leaves
Orange wedges for garnish
Parsley or cilantro for garnish

1. Combine salt and pepper; rub over chicken. Arrange chicken, breast side up, in 13×9-inch baking pan. Bake, uncovered, 30 minutes.

2. In medium saucepan, combine marmalade, butter, onion, garlic and thyme. Heat 1 to 2 minutes, stirring frequently. Baste chicken with marmalade mixture 2 to 3 times.

3. Bake, uncovered, 15 to 20 minutes or until chicken is no longer pink in center and juices run clear. Remove from oven. Discard remaining marmalade mixture. Garnish with orange wedges, parsley or cilantro. *Makes 4 to 6 servings*

Herbed Turkey Breast with Orange Sauce

1 large onion, chopped
3 cloves garlic, minced
1 teaspoon dried rosemary
½ teaspoon black pepper
2 to 3 pounds boneless skinless turkey breast
1½ cups orange juice

Slow Cooker Directions

1. Place onion in slow cooker. Combine garlic, rosemary and pepper in small bowl; set aside. Cut slices about three fourths of the way through turkey at 2-inch intervals. Rub garlic mixture between slices.

2. Place turkey, cut side up, in slow cooker. Pour orange juice over turkey. Cover; cook on LOW 7 to 8 hours or until turkey is no longer pink in center.

Makes 4 to 6 servings

Roast Capon with Fruit and Nut Stuffing

4 tablespoons butter or margarine, divided
1 tart apple, diced
½ cup chopped golden raisins or dried cranberries
¼ cup sliced green onions
¼ cup chopped celery
4 cups stale bread cubes
2 tablespoons chopped fresh parsley *or* 1 teaspoon dried parsley
2 teaspoons poultry seasoning
1 teaspoon salt
½ teaspoon black pepper
1½ cups fat-free reduced-sodium chicken broth
½ cup dry sherry
½ cup toasted slivered almonds
¼ cup honey
2 tablespoons mustard
½ teaspoon curry powder
1 capon (8 to 9 pounds)
¼ cup water
¼ cup all-purpose flour

Preheat oven to 325°F. For stuffing, melt 2 tablespoons butter in skillet over medium-high heat. Add apple, raisins, green onions and celery; cook and stir 3 minutes or until fruit is tender. Add bread cubes; toss. Add parsley, poultry seasoning, salt and pepper; toss. Add chicken broth, sherry and almonds; toss until combined.

For glaze
Bring honey, remaining 2 tablespoons butter, mustard and curry powder to a boil in saucepan over medium-high heat. Boil 1 minute; remove from heat.

Remove giblets and neck from capon; reserve for another use. Rinse capon under cold water and pat dry with paper towels. Stuff cavity loosely with about 3 cups stuffing (place remaining stuffing in greased baking dish). Tie legs together with wet cotton string and place, breast side up, on rack in shallow roasting pan coated with nonstick cooking spray. Insert meat thermometer into meaty part of thigh not touching bone. Bake 3 hours or until meat thermometer registers 170°F, brushing well with glaze every 30 minutes. Loosely cover remaining stuffing. Place in oven during last 45 minutes of baking time.

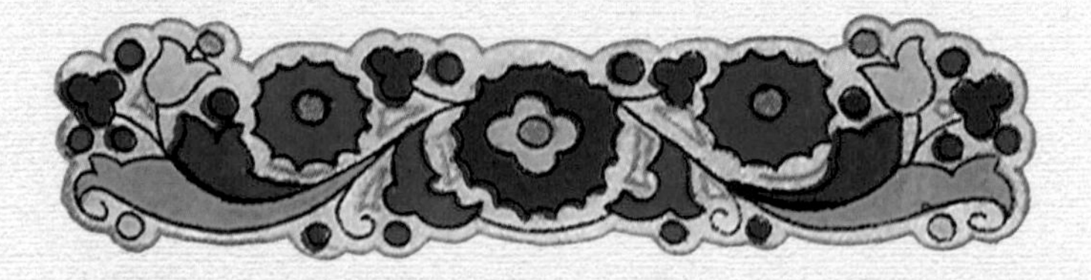

Transfer capon to platter. Remove stuffing from cavity and add to remaining stuffing. Cover capon with aluminum foil; let stand 10 minutes before carving.

For gravy

Strain pan juices into 2-cup glass measure; skim off fat. Add enough water to pan juices to equal 2 cups. Pour pan juice mixture into saucepan and place over medium heat. Combine 1/4 cup water and flour; stir until smooth. Gradually whisk flour mixture into saucepan; bring to a boil. Reduce heat to medium-low; simmer 2 to 3 minutes or until thickened. Season to taste. Serve with capon and stuffing.

Makes 8 servings

New England Roast Turkey

¼ cup butter
1 large onion, coarsely chopped
4 ribs celery, sliced
1 Granny Smith apple, coarsely chopped
1 package (about 11 ounces) diced dried fruit mix
¾ cup slivered almonds
⅓ cup chopped fresh parsley
⅛ teaspoon ground cloves
Salt and black pepper
1 whole turkey (12 to 14 pounds)
6 medium sweet potatoes, peeled and cut into 1-inch pieces
8 large carrots, thickly sliced
5 large shallot cloves, peeled
½ cup dry white wine

Preheat oven to 325°F. Melt butter in large saucepan over medium-low heat. Add onion; cook and stir 8 minutes or until tender. Remove from heat; stir in celery, apple, dried fruit, almonds, parsley and cloves. Add salt and pepper to taste.

Place fruit mixture in turkey cavity. Tie turkey legs together with kitchen string. Place turkey, breast side down, on rack in large oiled roasting pan. Season with salt and pepper, if desired. Add ½ cup water to pan. Bake, uncovered, 1½ hours.

Remove turkey from roasting pan; remove rack. Place turkey breast side up in roasting pan. Arrange sweet potatoes, carrots and shallots around turkey; season with salt and pepper, if desired. Baste turkey with pan juices. Add wine to roasting pan. Bake 2 to 2½ hours or until turkey is tender and thermometer inserted in thickest part of thigh registers 180°F, basting every 30 minutes.

Transfer turkey to cutting board; tent with foil. Let stand 10 minutes before carving. Drain vegetables and place in food processor; process until smooth. Place fruit stuffing from turkey cavity in serving bowl. Serve turkey with vegetable purée and fruit stuffing.

Makes 12 servings

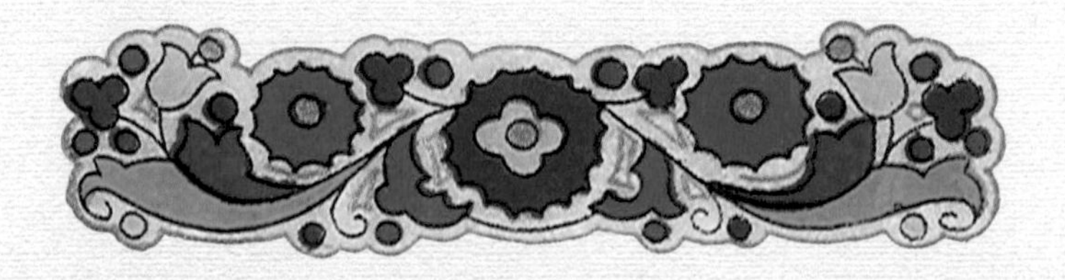

Chicken Marsala

1 tablespoon butter
2 boneless skinless chicken breasts, halved
1 cup sliced carrots
1 cup sliced fresh mushrooms
⅓ cup chicken broth
⅓ cup HOLLAND HOUSE® Marsala Cooking Wine

Melt butter in skillet over medium-high heat. Add chicken; cook 5 minutes. Turn chicken over, add remaining ingredients. Bring to a boil; simmer 15 to 20 minutes until juices run clear. Serve over cooked fettuccine, if desired. *Makes 4 servings*

Lemon-Herb Roast Chicken

⅓ cup lemon juice
¼ cup HOLLAND HOUSE® Vermouth Cooking Wine
¼ cup oil
½ teaspoon dried rosemary leaves
½ teaspoon dried thyme leaves
1 garlic clove, minced
1 whole chicken (2½ to 3 pounds)

1. In large plastic bowl, combine lemon juice, cooking wine, oil, rosemary, thyme and garlic; mix well. Add chicken, turning to coat all sides. Cover; refrigerate 1 to 2 hours, turning several times.

2. Heat oven to 375°F. Remove chicken from marinade; reserving marinade. Twist wing tips under back. Place chicken, breast side up, on rack in shallow pan. Brush with marinade. Roast 55 to 65 minutes, or until chicken is tender and juices run clear, brushing with marinade* halfway through roasting. Remove chicken to cutting board; let stand 5 to 10 minutes before carving. *Makes 4 servings*

**Do not baste during last 5 minutes of cooking.*

Turkey 'n' Stuffing Pie

1¼ cups water*
¼ cup butter or margarine*
3½ cups seasoned stuffing crumbs*
1⅓ cups *French's*® French Fried Onions
1 can (10¾ ounces) condensed cream of celery soup
¾ cup milk
1½ cups (7 ounces) cubed cooked turkey
1 package (10 ounces) frozen peas, thawed and drained

**3 cups leftover stuffing may be substituted for water, butter and stuffing crumbs. If stuffing is dry, stir in water, 1 tablespoon at a time, until moist but not wet.*

Preheat oven to 350°F. In medium saucepan, heat water and butter; stir until butter melts. Remove from heat. Stir in seasoned stuffing crumbs and ⅔ *cup* French Fried Onions. Spoon stuffing mixture into 9-inch round or fluted baking dish. Press stuffing evenly across bottom and up sides of dish to form a shell. In medium bowl, combine soup, milk, turkey and peas; pour into stuffing shell. Bake, covered, at 350°F for 30 minutes or until heated through. Top with remaining ⅔ *cup* onions; bake, uncovered, 5 minutes or until onions are golden brown.

Makes 4 to 6 servings

Microwave Directions: In 9-inch round or fluted microwave-safe dish, place water and butter. Cook, covered, on HIGH 3 minutes or until butter melts. Stir in stuffing crumbs and ⅔ *cup* onions. Press stuffing mixture into dish as above. Reduce milk to ½ cup. In large microwave-safe bowl, combine soup, milk, turkey and peas; cook, covered, 8 minutes. Stir turkey mixture halfway through cooking time. Pour turkey mixture into stuffing shell. Cook, uncovered, 4 to 6 minutes or until heated through. Rotate dish halfway through cooking time. Top with remaining ⅔ *cup* onions; cook, uncovered, 1 minute. Let stand 5 minutes.

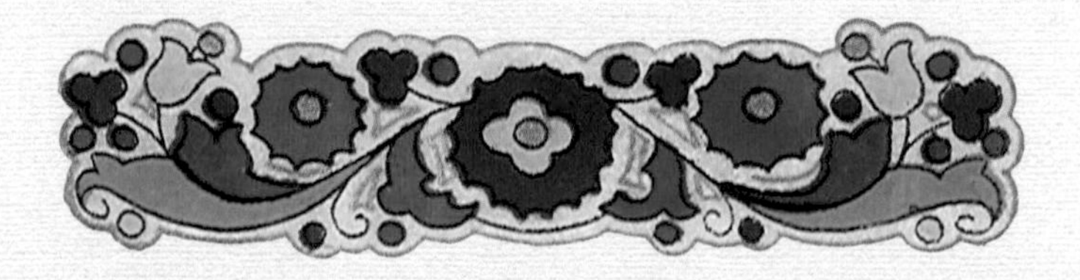

Roast Turkey Breast with Apple Corn Bread Stuffing

- Nonstick cooking spray
- 1 medium onion, chopped
- 1¼ cups reduced-sodium chicken broth
- 1 package (8 ounces) corn bread stuffing mix
- 1 Granny Smith apple, diced
- ¾ teaspoon dried sage, divided
- ¾ teaspoon dried thyme leaves, divided
- 1 (1½ pounds) boneless turkey breast
- 1 teaspoon paprika
- ¼ teaspoon black pepper
- 1 cup whole berry cranberry sauce (optional)

1. Preheat oven to 450°F. Coat 1½ quart casserole with cooking spray; set aside. Coat large saucepan with cooking spray; heat over medium heat. Add onion; cook and stir 5 minutes. Add broth; bring to a simmer. Stir in stuffing mix, apple, ¼ teaspoon sage and ¼ teaspoon thyme. Transfer mixture to prepared casserole; set aside.

2. Coat a shallow roasting pan with cooking spray. Place turkey breast in pan, skin side up; coat with cooking spray. Mix paprika, remaining ½ teaspoon sage, ½ teaspoon thyme and pepper in small bowl; sprinkle over turkey. Spray lightly with cooking spray.

3. Place turkey in preheated oven; roast 15 minutes. *Reduce oven temperature to 350°F.* Place stuffing in oven alongside turkey; continue to roast 35 minutes or until internal temperature of turkey reaches 170°F when tested with meat thermometer inserted into the thickest part of breast. Transfer turkey to cutting board; cover with foil and let stand 10 to 15 minutes before carving. Internal temperature will rise 5°F to 10°F during stand time. Remove stuffing from oven; cover to keep warm. Carve turkey into thin slices; serve with stuffing and cranberry sauce, if desired.

Makes 6 servings

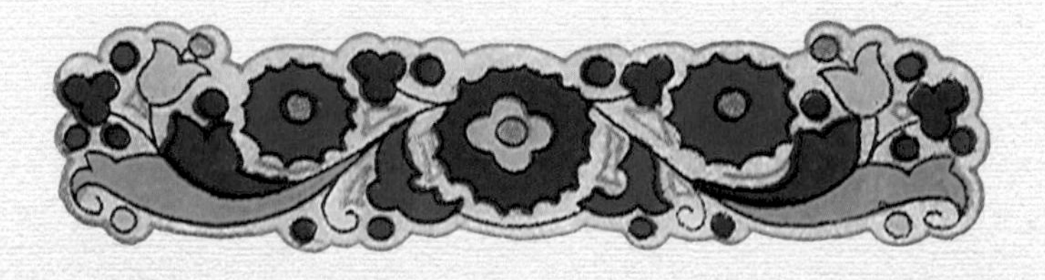

Broccoli-Filled Chicken Roulade

2 cups broccoli flowerets
1 tablespoon water
¼ cup fresh parsley
1 cup diced red bell pepper
4 ounces fat-free cream cheese, softened
2 tablespoons grated Parmesan cheese
2 tablespoons lemon juice
2 tablespoons olive oil
1 teaspoon paprika
¼ teaspoon salt
1 egg
½ cup skim milk
4 cups cornflakes, crushed
1 tablespoon dried basil leaves
8 boneless skinless chicken breast halves

1. Place broccoli and water in microwavable dish; cover. Microwave at HIGH 2 minutes. Let stand, covered, 2 minutes. Drain water from broccoli. Place broccoli in food processor or blender. Add parsley; process 10 seconds, scraping side of bowl if necessary. Add bell pepper, cream cheese, Parmesan cheese, lemon juice, oil, paprika and salt. Pulse 2 to 3 times or until bell pepper is minced.

2. Preheat oven to 375°F. Spray 11×7-inch baking pan with nonstick cooking spray. Lightly beat egg in small bowl. Add milk; blend well. Place cornflake crumbs in shallow bowl. Add basil; blend well.

3. Pound chicken breasts between two pieces of plastic wrap to ¼-inch thickness using flat side of meat mallet or rolling pin. Spread each chicken breast with ⅛ of the broccoli mixture, spreading to within ½ inch of edges. Roll up chicken breast from short end, tucking in sides if possible; secure with wooden picks. Dip roulades in milk mixture; roll in cornflake crumb mixture. Place in prepared baking pan. Bake 20 minutes or until chicken is no longer pink in center and juices run clear. Cut into slices, if desired.

Makes 8 servings

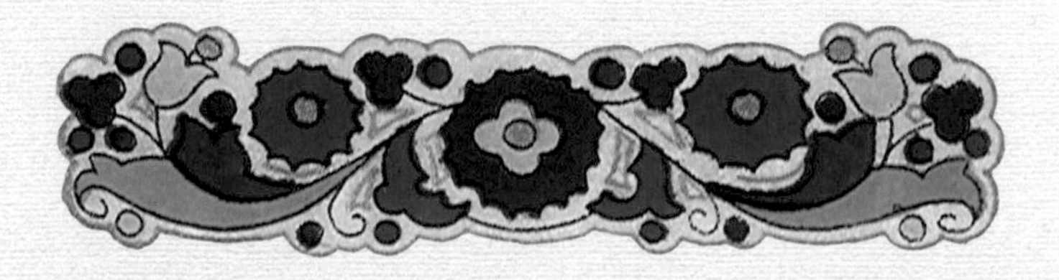

Broccoli-Filled Chicken Roulade

Turkey Breast with Southwestern Corn Bread Dressing

- 5 cups coarsely crumbled prepared corn bread
- 4 English muffins, coarsely crumbled
- 3 Anaheim chilies*, roasted, peeled, seeded and chopped
- 1 red bell pepper, roasted, peeled, seeded and chopped
- ¾ cup pine nuts, toasted
- 1 tablespoon chopped fresh cilantro
- 1 tablespoon chopped fresh parsley
- 1½ teaspoons chopped fresh basil *or* 1 teaspoon dried basil leaves
- 1½ teaspoons chopped fresh thyme *or* 1 teaspoon dried thyme leaves
- 1½ teaspoons chopped fresh oregano *or* 1 teaspoon dried oregano leaves
- 1 pound Italian turkey sausage
- 3 cups chopped celery
- 1 cup chopped onions
- 2 to 4 tablespoons chicken or turkey broth
- 1 bone-in turkey breast (5 to 6 pounds)
- 2 tablespoons minced garlic
- ½ cup chopped fresh cilantro

**Canned mild green chilies may be substituted.*

1. Preheat oven to 325°F. In large bowl combine corn bread, muffins, chilies, bell pepper, pine nuts, 1 tablespoon cilantro, parsley, basil, thyme and oregano; set aside.

2. In large skillet, over medium-high heat, cook and stir turkey sausage, celery and onions 8 to 10 minutes or until sausage is no longer pink and vegetables are tender. Add to corn bread mixture. Add broth if mixture is too dry; set aside.

3. Loosen skin on both sides of turkey breast, being careful not to tear skin, and leaving it connected at breast bone. Spread 1 tablespoon garlic under loosened skin over each breast half. Repeat procedure, spreading ¼ cup cilantro over each breast half.

4. Place turkey breast in 13×9×2-inch roasting pan lightly coated with nonstick cooking spray. Spoon half of stuffing mixture under breast cavity. Spoon remaining stuffing into 2-quart casserole lightly coated with nonstick cooking spray; set aside. Roast turkey breast, uncovered, 2 to 2½ hours or until meat thermometer registers 170°F in deepest portion of breast. Bake remaining stuffing, uncovered, during last 45 minutes.

Makes 12 servings

Favorite recipe from National Turkey Federation

Roast Turkey with Honey Cranberry Relish

1 medium orange
12 ounces fresh or frozen whole cranberries
¾ cup honey
2 pounds sliced roasted turkey breast

Quarter and slice unpeeled orange, removing seeds. Coarsely chop orange and cranberries. Place in medium saucepan and stir in honey. Bring to a boil over medium-high heat. Cook 3 to 4 minutes; cool. Serve over turkey. *Makes 8 servings*

Favorite recipe from National Honey Board

Chicken & Broccoli with Garlic Sauce

2 tablespoons olive or vegetable oil
4 boneless, skinless chicken breast halves (about 1¼ pounds)
1 package (10 ounces) frozen broccoli florets, thawed
1 envelope LIPTON® RECIPE SECRETS® Savory Herb with Garlic Soup Mix
1 cup water
3 tablespoons orange juice
1 teaspoon soy sauce

1. In 12-inch nonstick skillet, heat oil over medium-high heat and brown chicken. Remove chicken and set aside.

2. In same skillet, add broccoli and soup mix blended with water, orange juice and soy sauce. Bring to a boil over high heat.

3. Return chicken to skillet. Reduce heat to low and simmer covered 10 minutes or until chicken is no longer pink. Serve, if desired, over hot cooked rice.

Makes 4 servings

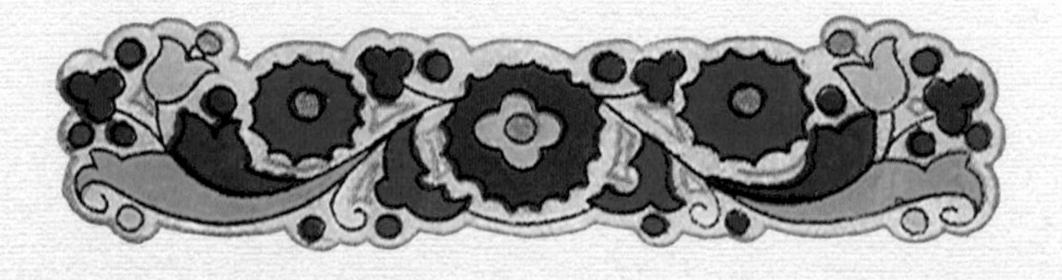

Quick Chicken Pot Pie

- 1 pound boneless skinless chicken thighs, cut into 1-inch cubes
- 1 can (about 14 ounces) chicken broth
- 3 tablespoons all-purpose flour
- 2 tablespoons butter, softened
- 1 package (10 ounces) frozen mixed vegetables, thawed
- 1 can (about 4 ounces) button mushrooms, drained
- ¼ teaspoon dried basil leaves
- ¼ teaspoon dried oregano leaves
- ¼ teaspoon dried thyme leaves
- 1 cup biscuit baking mix
- 6 tablespoons milk

1. Preheat oven to 450°F. Place chicken and broth in large skillet; cover and bring to a boil over high heat. Reduce heat to medium; simmer, uncovered, 5 minutes or until chicken is tender.

2. While chicken is cooking, mix flour and butter; set aside. Combine mixed vegetables, mushrooms, basil, oregano and thyme in greased 2-quart casserole.

3. Add flour mixture to chicken and broth in skillet; stir with wire whisk until smooth. Cook and stir until thickened. Add to vegetable mixture; mix well.

4. Blend biscuit mix and milk in medium bowl until smooth. Drop 4 scoops batter onto chicken mixture.

5. Bake 18 to 20 minutes or until biscuits are browned and casserole is hot and bubbly.

Makes 4 servings

Tip: This dish can be prepared through step 3 covered and refrigerated up to 24 hours, if desired, proceed with step 4. Bake as directed for 20 to 25 minutes.

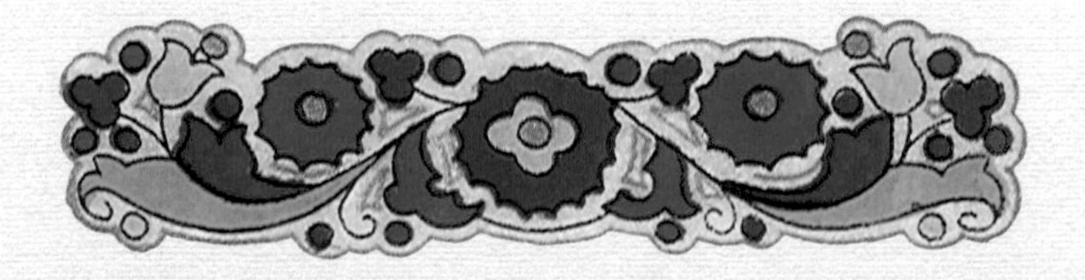

Spinach-Stuffed Chicken Breasts

2 boneless skinless chicken breasts (8 ounces each), halved
5 ounces frozen chopped spinach, thawed and well drained
2 tablespoons freshly grated Parmesan cheese
1 teaspoon grated lemon peel
¼ teaspoon black pepper
Olive oil-flavored nonstick cooking spray
1 cup thinly sliced mushrooms
6 slices (2 ounces) thinly sliced low fat turkey-ham
1 cup white grape juice

1. Trim fat from chicken; discard. Place each chicken breast between 2 sheets of plastic wrap. Pound with meat mallet until chicken is about ¼ inch thick.

2. Preheat oven to 350°F. Pat spinach dry with paper towels. Combine spinach, Parmesan, lemon peel and black pepper in large bowl. Spray small nonstick skillet with cooking spray; add mushrooms. Cook and stir over medium heat 3 to 4 minutes or until tender.

3. Arrange 1½ slices turkey-ham over each chicken breast. Spread each with one-fourth of spinach mixture. Top each with mushrooms. Beginning with longer side, roll chicken tightly. Tie with kitchen string.

4. Place stuffed chicken breasts in 9-inch square baking pan, seam side down. Lightly spray chicken with cooking spray. Pour white grape juice over top. Bake 30 minutes or until chicken is no longer pink.

5. Remove string; cut chicken rolls into ½-inch diagonal slices. Arrange on plate. Pour pan juices over chicken. Garnish as desired.

Makes 4 servings

Yuletide Desserts

Cran-Raspberry Hazelnut Trifle

2 cups hazelnut-flavored liquid dairy creamer
1 package (3.4 ounces) instant vanilla pudding and pie filling mix
1 package (about 11 ounces) frozen pound cake, thawed
1 can (21 ounces) raspberry pie filling
1 can (16 ounces) whole berry cranberry sauce

1. Combine dairy creamer and pudding mix in medium bowl; beat with wire whisk 1 to 2 minutes or until thickened.

2. Cut pound cake into 3/4-inch cubes. Combine pie filling and cranberry sauce in medium bowl; blend well.

3. Layer 1/3 of cake cubes, 1/4 of fruit sauce and 1/3 of pudding mixture in 1 1/2- to 2-quart straight-sided glass serving bowl. Repeat layers twice; top with remaining fruit sauce. Cover; refrigerate until serving time. *Makes 8 servings*

Serve it with Style!: Garnish trifle with whipped topping and fresh mint sprigs.

Prep Time: 20 minutes

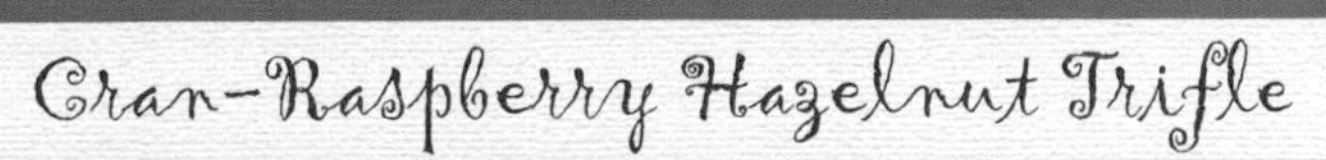

Oregon Hot Apple Cider

8 cups apple cider
½ cup dried cherries
½ cup dried cranberries
3 cinnamon sticks, broken in half
8 whole cloves
1 pear, quartered, cored, sliced

1. Combine cider, cherries, cranberries, cinnamon sticks and cloves in large saucepan. Heat just to a simmer; do not boil.

2. Add pear before serving. *Makes 16 (½-cup) servings*

Creamy Holiday Tarts

1 (4-serving-size) package vanilla flavor instant pudding and pie filling mix
1 (14-ounce) can sweetened condensed milk
¾ cup raisins
¾ cup cold water
1 teaspoon ground nutmeg
1 teaspoon brandy extract
1 cup whipping cream, whipped, divided
2 (4-ounce) packages READY CRUST® Mini-Graham Cracker Crusts
Additional raisins and ground nutmeg, for garnish

1. Mix together pudding mix, sweetened condensed milk, raisins, water, nutmeg and brandy extract in large bowl. Chill 15 minutes.

2. Fold 1 cup whipped cream into pudding mixture. Spoon into crusts.

3. Garnish with remaining whipped cream. Sprinkle with additional raisins and nutmeg. Refrigerate leftovers. *Makes 12 servings*

Prep Time: 10 minutes

Spiced Pear with Vanilla Ice Cream

1 sheet (18×12 inches) heavy-duty foil
2 teaspoons butter, softened
1 tablespoon light brown sugar
¼ teaspoon pumpkin pie spice
1 large Bosc pear, halved lengthwise and cored
Lemon juice
2 scoops vanilla ice cream

1. Preheat oven to 450°F. Coat center of foil with butter.

2. Combine sugar and pumpkin pie spice in small bowl. Sprinkle sugar mixture over butter. Sprinkle cut sides of pear halves with lemon juice. Place pear halves, cut side down, side by side on sugar mixture.

3. Double fold sides and ends of foil to seal foil packet, leaving headspace for heat circulation. Place packet on baking sheet.

4. Bake 40 minutes or until pear halves are tender. Remove from oven. Let stand 15 minutes.

5. Open packet and transfer pear halves to serving plates. Spoon sauce over pears. Serve with ice cream.

Makes 2 servings

Baked Apples

2 tablespoons sugar
2 tablespoons GRANDMA'S® Molasses
2 tablespoons raisins, chopped
2 tablespoons chopped walnuts
6 apples, cored

Heat oven to 350°F. In medium bowl, combine sugar, molasses, raisins and walnuts. Fill apple cavities with molasses mixture. Place in 13×9-inch baking dish. Pour ½ cup hot water over the apples and bake 25 minutes or until soft.

Makes 6 servings

French Yule Log

Powdered sugar
4 eggs, separated
¾ cup granulated sugar, divided
¾ cup ground blanched almonds
⅓ cup all-purpose flour
⅓ cup HERSHEY'S Cocoa
½ teaspoon baking soda
¼ teaspoon salt
¼ cup water
1 teaspoon vanilla extract
¼ teaspoon almond extract
Whipped Cream Filling (recipe page 237)
Creamy Cocoa Log Frosting (recipe page 237)

1. Heat oven to 375°F. Line 15×10½-inch jelly-roll pan with foil; generously grease foil. Sift powdered sugar onto clean towel.

2. Beat egg yolks in medium bowl 3 minutes on medium speed of mixer. Gradually add ½ cup granulated sugar, beating another 2 minutes until thick and lemon-colored. Combine almonds, flour, cocoa, baking soda and salt; add alternately with water to egg yolk mixture, beating on low speed just until blended. Stir in vanilla and almond extracts.

3. Beat egg whites in large bowl until foamy. Gradually add ¼ cup granulated sugar, beating until stiff peaks form. Carefully fold chocolate mixture into beaten egg whites. Spread batter evenly into prepared pan.

4. Bake 16 to 18 minutes or until top springs back when lightly touched. Cool in pan on wire rack 10 minutes; remove from pan onto prepared towel. Carefully remove foil. Cool completely.

5. Cut into four equal rectangles approximately 3½×10 inches. Chill layers while preparing filling and frosting. Place one cake layer on serving plate. Spread one-third (about 1 cup) Whipped Cream Filling evenly over cake layer; top with another cake layer. Repeat with remaining cake and filling, ending with cake layer. Refrigerate about 1 hour before frosting. Generously frost loaf with Creamy Cocoa Log Frosting. Swirl frosting with spatula or score with fork to resemble bark. Refrigerate at least 4 hours before serving. Garnish with shaved chocolate and holly, if desired. Cover; refrigerate leftover dessert. *Makes 10 to 12 servings*

Whipped Cream Filling

1½ cups cold whipping cream
⅓ cup powdered sugar
1 teaspoon vanilla extract

Combine whipping cream, powdered sugar and vanilla in large bowl. Beat until cream is stiff. (Do not overbeat.) *Makes about 3 cups filling*

Creamy Cocoa Frosting

3½ cups powdered sugar
½ cup HERSHEY'S Cocoa
½ cup (1 stick) butter or margarine, softened
2 tablespoons light corn syrup
2 teaspoons vanilla extract
⅓ cup milk

Combine powdered sugar and cocoa. Beat butter, ½ cup cocoa mixture, corn syrup and vanilla in medium bowl until smooth. Add remaining cocoa mixture alternately with milk, beating until smooth and of spreading consistency. *Makes 2½ cups frosting*

Hidden Pumpkin Pie

1½ cups canned solid-pack pumpkin
1 cup evaporated fat-free milk
½ cup cholesterol-free egg substitute
¼ cup no-calorie sweetener
1 teaspoon pumpkin pie spice
1¼ teaspoons vanilla, divided
3 egg whites
¼ teaspoon cream of tartar
⅓ cup honey

1. Preheat oven to 350°F.

2. Stir together pumpkin, evaporated milk, egg substitute, sweetener, pumpkin pie spice and 1 teaspoon vanilla. Pour into 6 (6-ounce) custard cups or 6 (3/4-cup) soufflé dishes. Place in shallow baking dish or pan. Pour boiling water around custard cups or soufflé dishes to depth of 1 inch. Bake 25 minutes.

3. Meanwhile, beat egg whites, cream of tartar and remaining 1/4 teaspoon vanilla on high speed of electric mixer until soft peaks form. Gradually add honey; continue beating on high speed until stiff peaks form.

4. Spread egg white mixture on top of hot pumpkin mixture. Return to oven. Bake 15 to 16 minutes or until tops are golden brown. Let stand 10 minutes. Serve warm.

Makes 6 servings

Holiday Egg Nog Punch

2 (1-quart) cans BORDEN® Egg Nog, chilled
1 (12-ounce) can frozen orange juice concentrate, thawed
1 cup cold water
Orange sherbet

1. In large pitcher combine all ingredients except sherbet; mix well.

2. Just before serving, pour into punch bowl; top with scoops of sherbet. Refrigerate leftovers.

Makes about 1 quart

Prep Time: 5 minutes

Mocha Nog

1 quart eggnog
1 tablespoon instant French vanilla or regular coffee granules
¼ cup coffee-flavored liqueur

1. Heat eggnog and coffee granules in large saucepan over medium heat until mixture is hot and coffee granules are dissolved; do not boil. Remove from heat; stir in coffee liqueur.

2. Pour eggnog into individual mugs. *Makes 8 servings*

Prep and Cook Time: 10 minutes

Cinnamon-Raisin-Apple Bread Pudding

1 large Granny Smith apple, peeled and cut into ½-inch chunks
¾ cup plus 2 tablespoons sugar, divided
1 teaspoon cinnamon
3½ cups diced cinnamon-raisin bread (about eight slices)
3 eggs
2 cups milk
¼ cup butter, melted and cooled
¼ teaspoon salt
Prepared caramel or butterscotch sauce, warmed

1. Preheat oven to 350°F. Grease 1½ quart baking dish; set aside. Combine apple, 2 tablespoons sugar and cinnamon in large bowl; mix well. Add bread cubes; toss to combine. Transfer mixture into prepared dish.

2. Beat eggs lightly in medium bowl. Add remaining ¾ cup sugar; beat well. Stir in milk, butter and salt; mix well. Pour over bread mixture. Press down so that bread is coated with milk mixture. Let stand 10 minutes (or cover and refrigerate overnight).

3. Bake about 50 minutes or until puffed and golden brown. Cool on wire rack at least 20 minutes. Serve warm or at room temperature with caramel sauce.

Makes 6 to 8 servings

Cranberry Cobbler

2 (16-ounce) cans sliced peaches in light syrup, drained
1 (16-ounce) can whole berry cranberry sauce
1 package DUNCAN HINES® Cinnamon Swirl Muffin Mix
½ cup chopped pecans
⅓ cup butter or margarine, melted
Whipped topping or ice cream

1. Preheat oven to 350°F.

2. Cut peach slices in half lengthwise. Combine peach slices and cranberry sauce in *ungreased* 9-inch square pan. Knead swirl packet from Mix for 10 seconds. Squeeze contents evenly over fruit.

3. Combine muffin mix, contents of topping packet from Mix and pecans in large bowl. Add melted butter. Stir until thoroughly blended (mixture will be crumbly). Sprinkle crumbs over fruit. Bake 40 to 45 minutes or until lightly browned and bubbly. Serve warm with whipped topping. *Makes 9 servings*

Tip: Store leftovers in the refrigerator. Reheat in microwave oven to serve warm.

Holiday Chocolate Parfaits

1 box (4-serving size) sugar-free instant chocolate pudding mix
2 cups fat-free (skim) milk
4 sugar-free chocolate sandwich cookies, finely crushed
8 tablespoons thawed frozen light nondairy whipped topping
4 teaspoons multi-colored sprinkles

1. Prepare pudding according to package directions using 2 cups milk.

2. Layer half of pudding in 4 parfait glasses or clear plastic cups. Spread 1 tablespoon whipped topping over pudding in each glass. Sprinkle with ½ of crushed cookies. Layer remaining pudding over top of cookies. Garnish with remaining whipped topping, cookies and sprinkles. *Makes 4 servings*

Pumpkin-Cranberry Custard

1 can (30 ounces) pumpkin pie filling
1 can (12 ounces) evaporated milk
1 cup dried cranberries
4 eggs, beaten
1 cup crushed or whole ginger snap cookies (optional)
Whipped cream (optional)

Slow Cooker Directions
Combine pumpkin, evaporated milk, cranberries and eggs in slow cooker and mix thoroughly. Cover and cook on HIGH 4 to $4^1/_2$ hours. Serve with crushed or whole ginger snaps and whipped cream, if desired. *Make 4 to 6 servings*

Old-Fashioned Caramel Apples

1 package (14 ounces) caramels, unwrapped
2 tablespoons water
6 medium Granny Smith apples
6 wooden craft sticks
Chopped toasted pecans, walnuts or roasted peanuts
Orange and black jimmies or sprinkles

1. Place caramels and water in a medium heavy saucepan. Cook over medium-low heat until melted and very hot, stirring frequently.

2. Insert stick into stem end of each apple. Place pecans in shallow bowl and jimmies in another shallow bowl. Dip apple into caramel, tilting saucepan until apple is coated; let excess caramel drip back in saucepan. Remove excess caramel by scraping bottom of apple across rim of saucepan. Immediately roll apple in pecans and/or jimmies. Place, stick side up, on baking sheet lined with waxed paper. Repeat with remaining apples. Rewarm caramel, if needed. Chill apples at least 10 minutes or until caramel is firm before serving. *Makes 6 servings*

Gingered Pumpkin Custard

¾ cup sugar
2 eggs
1½ teaspoons ground cinnamon
½ teaspoon salt
½ teaspoon nutmeg
1 can (15 ounces) solid-pack pumpkin
1¼ cups half-and-half
3 tablespoons chopped candied ginger
Sweetened whipped cream
Halloween sprinkles or candy corn

1. Preheat oven to 375°F. Grease 1½ quart oval casserole dish or 8-inch glass baking dish.

2. Combine sugar, eggs, cinnamon, salt and nutmeg in medium bowl; mix well. Add pumpkin and cream. Mix until well blended. Pour into prepared dish. Sprinkle ginger evenly over top of pumpkin mixture.

3. Bake 45 minutes or until knife inserted in center comes out clean. Cool on wire rack at least 20 minutes before serving. Serve warm or at room temperature, garnished with whipped cream and sprinkles. *Makes 6 to 8 servings*

Variation: For individual servings, pour custard mixture into 6 or 8 ramekins or custard cups. Place on a baking sheet. Bake until knife inserted in center comes out clean, 35 to 40 minutes.

Baked Pear Dessert

2 tablespoons dried cranberries or raisins
1 tablespoon toasted sliced almonds
⅛ teaspoon cinnamon
⅓ cup unsweetened apple cider or apple juice, divided
1 medium unpeeled pear, cut in half lengthwise and cored
½ cup vanilla sugar-free low-fat frozen ice cream or frozen yogurt

1. Preheat oven to 350°F. Combine cranberries, almonds, cinnamon and 1 teaspoon cider in small bowl.

2. Place pear halves, cut side up, in small baking dish. Mound almond mixture on top of pear halves. Pour remaining cider into dish. Cover with foil.

3. Bake pear halves 35 to 40 minutes or until pears are soft, spooning cider in dish over pears once or twice during baking. Serve warm and top with ice cream.

Makes 2 servings

Cranberry Crunch Gelatin

1 package (3 ounces) cherry-flavored gelatin mix, plus ingredients to prepare
1 can (16 ounces) whole cranberry sauce
1 cup miniature marshmallows
1 cup coarsely chopped English walnuts

Prepare gelatin according to package directions. Chill until slightly set, about 2 hours.

Thoroughly fold in remaining ingredients. Chill until firm about 2 to 3 hours.

Makes 6 servings

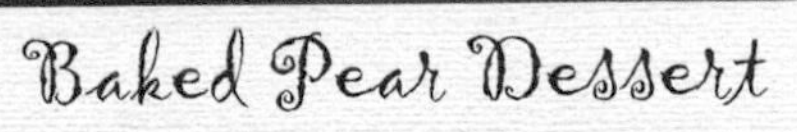

Baked Pear Dessert

Walnut Tartlets with Chocolate Ganache Filling

Chocolate Leaves (recipe page 251)
½ cup walnut halves, toasted
1 cup all-purpose flour
¼ cup sugar
1 tablespoon grated lemon peel
⅓ cup butter or margarine, cut into pieces
1 egg, lightly beaten
Chocolate Ganache (recipe page 251)

1. Prepare Chocolate Leaves. Set aside.

2. Place walnuts in food processor. Process using on/off pulsing action until walnuts are finely chopped, but not pasty.

3. Reserve 2 tablespoons walnuts. Place remaining walnuts in medium bowl. Add flour, sugar and lemon peel; blend well. Cut in butter with pastry blender or two knives until mixture resembles coarse crumbs. Stir in egg with fork until mixture holds together.

4. Spoon 2 teaspoonfuls mixture into *ungreased* mini-muffin cups. Press dough onto bottom and up side of each cup with fingers.

5. Bake 16 to 20 minutes or until golden brown. Cool 5 minutes in pan. Remove shells from pans. Cool completely on wire racks.

6. Prepare Chocolate Ganache. Spoon ½ teaspoon ganache into each shell. Sprinkle reserved 2 tablespoons chopped nuts evenly over shells. Gently push chocolate leaf into each shell.

7. Store tightly covered in refrigerator up to 1 week.

Makes 30 tartlets

Chocolate Leaves

½ cup (2 ounces) chopped semisweet chocolate or semisweet chocolate chips
1 teaspoon shortening
Assorted nontoxic fresh leaves such as rose, lemon or camellia,* cleaned and dried

**Nontoxic leaves are available in florist shops.*

1. Place large sheet heavy-duty foil on counter.

2. Fill saucepan ¼ full (about 1 inch deep) with warm water. Place chocolate and shortening in 1-cup glass measure. To melt chocolate, place measure in warm water; stir frequently with rubber spatula until smooth. (Be careful not to get any water into chocolate or chocolate may become lumpy.)

3. Brush melted chocolate onto underside of each leaf with small, clean craft paintbrush or pastry brush, coating leaf thickly and evenly. Carefully wipe off any chocolate that may have run onto front of leaf.

4. Place leaves, chocolate-sides up, on foil. Let stand 1 hour or until chocolate is set.

5. Carefully peel leaves away from chocolate beginning at stem ends; refrigerate chocolate leaves until ready to use.

Makes 30 to 40 leaves

Chocolate Ganache

2 tablespoons whipping cream
1 tablespoon butter
½ cup (2 ounces) chopped semisweet chocolate or semisweet chocolate chips
½ teaspoon vanilla

Heat whipping cream and butter in small saucepan over medium heat until butter melts and mixture boils, stirring frequently with wooden spoon. Remove saucepan from heat. Stir in chocolate and vanilla until mixture is smooth, returning to heat for 20 to 30 second intervals as needed to melt chocolate. Keep warm (ganache is semi-firm at room temperature).

Makes about ⅓ cup

Easy Cocoa Mix

2 cups nonfat dry milk powder
1 cup sugar
¾ cup powdered non-dairy creamer
½ cup unsweetened cocoa powder
¼ teaspoon salt

Combine all ingredients in small bowl until well blended. Spoon into1-quart airtight container or decorative gift jar; cover. *Makes about 4 cups mix or 16 servings*

For single serving: Place rounded 1/4 cup Easy Cocoa Mix in mug or cup; add 3/4 cup boiling water. Stir until mix is dissolved. Top with sweetened whipped cream and marshmallows, if desired. Serve immediately.

Cocoa Marshmallow Mix: Prepare Easy Cocoa Mix in 2-quart airtight container as directed, adding 1 package (10½ ounces) miniature marshmallows.

For single serving: Place rounded 1/2 cup Cocoa Marshmallow Mix in mug or cup; add 3/4 cup boiling water. Stir until mix is dissolved. Serve immediately.

Mocha Coffee Mix

1 cup nonfat dry milk powder
¾ cup granulated sugar
⅔ cup powdered non-dairy creamer
½ cup unsweetened cocoa powder
⅓ cup instant coffee, pressed through fine sieve
¼ cup packed brown sugar
1 teaspoon ground cinnamon
¼ teaspoon salt
¼ teaspoon ground nutmeg

Combine all ingredients in small bowl until well blended. Spoon into 1-quart airtight container or decorative gift jar; cover. *Makes about 3½ cups mix or 10 to 12 servings*

For single serving: Place rounded 1/4 cup Mocha Coffee Mix in mug or cup; add 3/4 cup boiling water. Stir until mix is dissolved. Serve immediately.

Cranberry-Apple Strudel

Butter-flavored nonstick cooking spray
1 tablespoon margarine
1 tablespoon packed light brown sugar
2 medium Golden Delicious apples, cored, peeled and diced
¼ cup raisins
1 can (16 ounces) whole-berry cranberry sauce
6 sheets phyllo dough
3 tablespoons graham cracker crumbs, divided
¼ cup toasted almonds, chopped

1. Preheat oven to 375°F. Spray baking sheet with cooking spray. Set aside. Melt margarine in large saucepan over medium heat. Add brown sugar; bring to a boil. Add apples and raisins; cook 10 minutes or until apples can be easily pierced with fork. Remove from heat. Add cranberry sauce; mix well. Set aside.

2. Place 1 sheet of phyllo on piece of parchment paper with narrow side farthest away. Spray phyllo with cooking spray; sprinkle ½ tablespoon graham cracker crumbs on phyllo. Overlap second sheet of phyllo over first sheet about 1 inch down from top. Spray with cooking spray; sprinkle with ½ tablespoon crumbs. Continue overlapping with remaining phyllo and crumbs, spraying with cooking spray between each layer.

3. Spoon cooled cranberry mixture into center of phyllo. Sprinkle chopped almonds over mixture. Fold bottom and sides of phyllo to cover mixture, forming an envelope. With floured hands, roll filled phyllo, jelly-roll fashion, starting to roll from long end, to form strudel. Place strudel on prepared cookie sheet. Spray top with cooking spray. Make 8 diagonal cuts across top of strudel. Bake 12 to 15 minutes or until lightly browned.

4. Cool on wire rack 30 minutes. Cut crosswise into 8 pieces. *Makes 8 servings*

Luscious Pecan Bread Pudding

3 cups French bread cubes
3 tablespoons chopped pecans, toasted
2¼ cups low-fat milk
2 eggs, beaten
½ cup sugar
1 teaspoon vanilla
¾ teaspoon ground cinnamon, divided
¾ cup reduced-calorie cranberry juice cocktail
1½ cups frozen pitted tart cherries
2 tablespoons sugar substitute

Slow Cooker Directions

1. Toss bread cubes and pecans in soufflé dish. Combine milk, eggs, sugar, vanilla and ½ teaspoon cinnamon in large bowl. Pour over bread mixture in soufflé dish. Cover tightly with foil. Make foil handles (see note). Place soufflé dish in slow cooker. Pour hot water into slow cooker to come about 1½ inches from top of soufflé dish. Cover and cook on LOW 2 to 3 hours.

2. Meanwhile, stir together cranberry juice and remaining ¼ teaspoon cinnamon in small saucepan; stir in frozen cherries. Bring sauce to a boil over medium heat, about 5 minutes. Remove from heat. Stir in sugar substitute. Lift dish from slow cooker with foil handles. Serve bread pudding with cherry sauce. *Makes 6 servings*

Foil Handles: Tear off three 18×2-inch strips of heavy foil or use regular foil folded to double thickness. Crisscross foil strips in spoke design and place in slow cooker to allow for easy removal of bread pudding.

White Chocolate Bavarian Christmas Tree

Ingredients

1 cup half-and-half
2 teaspoons vanilla
2 envelopes unflavored gelatin
6 eggs, separated*
12 ounces high-quality white or semisweet chocolate
1 teaspoon cream of tartar
1½ cups whipping cream, whipped
Decorations: Spearmint candy leaves, red cinnamon candies, red candy-coated licorice pieces, green miniature jaw breakers

Supplies

8-cup tree mold or other decorative mold

**Use only grade A clean, uncracked eggs.*

1. Combine half-and-half and vanilla in medium saucepan. Sprinkle gelatin over mixture; let stand 5 minutes. Stir over low heat until gelatin is completely dissolved.

2. Beat egg yolks in small bowl. Stir about ½ cup gelatin mixture into egg yolks; return egg yolk mixture to saucepan. Cook over low heat, stirring constantly, until thick enough to coat the back of a spoon.

3. Melt chocolate in top of double boiler over hot, not boiling, water, stirring constantly. Stir gelatin mixture into chocolate. Remove from heat; cool to room temperature.

4. Beat egg whites and cream of tartar until stiff peaks form. Gently fold cooled chocolate mixture into beaten egg whites. Fold in whipped cream.

5. Spoon mixture into 8-cup tree mold or other decorative mold. Refrigerate until set, 8 hours or overnight.

6. To unmold, pull chocolate mixture from edge of mold with moistened fingers. Or, run small metal spatula or pointed knife dipped in warm water around edge of mold. Dip bottom of mold briefly in warm water. Place serving plate on top of mold. Invert mold and plate and shake to loosen chocolate mixture. Gently remove mold. Decorate with candies.

Makes 12 to 14 servings

Almond-Pear Strudel

¾ cup slivered almonds, divided
5 to 6 cups thinly sliced crisp pears (4 to 5 medium pears)
1 tablespoon grated lemon peel
1 tablespoon lemon juice
⅓ cup plus 1 teaspoon sugar, divided
2 teaspoons ground cinnamon
1 teaspoon ground nutmeg
4 tablespoons melted butter or margarine, divided
6 sheets (¼ pound) phyllo dough
½ teaspoon almond extract

1. Preheat oven to 300°F. Spread almonds in shallow baking pan. Bake 10 to 12 minutes or until lightly browned, stirring frequently; cool and cover. Set aside.

2. Place sliced pears in large microwavable container. Stir in lemon peel and lemon juice. Microwave at HIGH 6 minutes or until tender; cool. Cover pears and refrigerate overnight. Combine 1/3 cup sugar, cinnamon and nutmeg in small bowl; cover and set aside.

3. Place butter in microwavable container. Microwave at HIGH 20 seconds or until melted. Lay 2 sheets plastic wrap on work surface to make 20-inch square. Place 1 phyllo sheet in middle of plastic wrap. (Cover remaining phyllo dough with damp kitchen towel to prevent dough from drying out.) Brush 1 teaspoon melted butter onto phyllo sheet. Place second phyllo sheet over first; brush with 1 teaspoon butter. Repeat layering with remaining sheets of phyllo. Cover with plastic wrap. Cover remaining butter. Refrigerate phyllo dough and butter overnight or up to 1 day.

4. Preheat oven to 400°F. Drain reserved pears in colander. Toss pears with reserved sugar mixture and almond extract. Melt reserved butter.

5. Uncover phyllo dough and spread pear mixture evenly over phyllo, leaving 3-inch strip on far long side. Sprinkle pear mixture with 1/2 cup toasted almonds. Brush strip with 2 teaspoons melted butter. Beginning at long side of phyllo opposite 3-inch strip, carefully roll up jelly-roll style, using plastic wrap to gently lift, forming strudel. Place strudel, seam side down, onto buttered baking sheet. Brush top with 1 teaspoon butter.

6. Bake 20 minutes or until deep golden. Brush again with 1 teaspoon butter. Combine remaining 1/4 cup toasted almonds with remaining butter; sprinkle on top of strudel. Sprinkle with remaining 1 teaspoon sugar. Bake an additional 5 minutes. Cool 10 minutes; sprinkle with powdered sugar, if desired. *Makes 8 servings*

Apple Cranberry Cobbler

6 medium Granny Smith apples, peeled, cored and thinly sliced
¾ cup dried cranberries or dried cherries
⅓ cup orange juice
⅔ cup packed light brown sugar
1½ cups plus 2 tablespoons all-purpose flour, divided
1¼ teaspoons ground cinnamon
¼ teaspoon ground cloves
¾ cup plus 1 teaspoon granulated sugar, divided
1½ teaspoons baking powder
1 egg
⅓ cup milk
¼ cup butter, melted
1 cup apple butter
2 tablespoons amaretto liqueur (optional)
Mint leaves (optional)

Preheat oven to 375°F. Place apples and cranberries in 11×7-inch baking dish. Drizzle orange juice over fruit.

Combine brown sugar, 2 tablespoons flour, cinnamon and cloves in small bowl. Pour over apple mixture; toss to coat.

Combine remaining 1½ cups flour, ¾ cup granulated sugar and baking powder in medium bowl. Add egg, milk and butter; stir to blend. Drop tablespoonfuls over top of apple mixture.

Sprinkle remaining 1 teaspoon granulated sugar over topping. Bake 35 minutes or until topping is lightly browned and apples are tender. Cool slightly in pan on wire rack.

Combine apple butter and liqueur, if desired, in small microwavable bowl. Microwave at HIGH 1 minute or until warm. Spoon 1 to 2 tablespoonfuls sauce over each serving. Garnish with mint leaves, if desired.

Makes 8 servings

Hot Buttered Cider

⅓ cup packed brown sugar
¼ cup butter or margarine, softened
¼ cup honey
¼ teaspoon ground cinnamon
¼ teaspoon ground nutmeg
Apple cider or juice

1. Beat sugar, butter, honey, cinnamon and nutmeg until well blended and fluffy. Place butter mixture in tightly covered container. Refrigerate up to 2 weeks. Bring butter mixture to room temperature before using.

2. To serve, heat apple cider in large saucepan over medium heat until hot. Fill individual mugs with hot apple cider; stir in 1 tablespoon batter per 1 cup apple cider.

Makes 12 servings

Prep and Cook Time: 15 minutes

Easy Egg Nog Pound Cake

1 (18.25-ounce) package yellow cake mix
1 (4-serving size) package instant vanilla pudding and pie filling mix
¾ cup BORDEN® Egg Nog
¾ cup vegetable oil
4 eggs
½ teaspoon ground nutmeg
Powdered sugar, if desired

1. Preheat oven to 350°F. In large mixing bowl, combine cake mix, pudding mix, Borden Egg Nog and oil; beat at low speed of electric mixer until moistened. Add eggs and nutmeg; beat at medium-high speed 4 minutes.

2. Pour into greased and floured 10-inch fluted or tube pan.

3. Bake 40 to 45 minutes or until wooden pick inserted near center comes out clean.

4. Cool 10 minutes; remove from pan. Cool completely. Sprinkle with powdered sugar, if desired.

Makes one 10-inch cake

Prep Time: 10 minutes
Bake Time: 40 to 45 minutes

Easy Egg Nog Pound Cake

Peppermint Ice Cream Pie

4 cups no-sugar-added vanilla ice cream
6 sugar-free peppermint candies
1 reduced-fat graham cracker pie crust
¼ cup sugar-free chocolate syrup

1. Scoop ice cream into medium bowl; let stand at room temperature 5 minutes or until softened, stirring occasionally.

2. Place candies in heavy-duty plastic food storage bag; coarsely crush with rolling pin or meat mallet. Stir candy into ice cream; spread evenly into pie crust.

3. Cover; freeze at least 4 hours or overnight. Using sharp knife that has been dipped into warm water, cut pie into slices. Transfer to serving plates; drizzle with chocolate.

Makes 12 servings

Autumn Gold Pumpkin Cake

1 package DUNCAN HINES® Moist Deluxe® Butter Recipe Golden Cake Mix
3 eggs
1 cup water
1 cup solid pack pumpkin
1½ teaspoons ground cinnamon, divided
¼ teaspoon ground ginger
¼ teaspoon ground nutmeg
1 cup chopped walnuts
1 container DUNCAN HINES® Vanilla Frosting
¼ cup coarsely chopped walnuts for garnish

1. Preheat oven to 375°F. Grease and flour two 8-inch round cake pans. Combine cake mix, eggs, water, pumpkin, 1 teaspoon cinnamon, ginger and nutmeg in large mixing bowl. Beat at medium speed with electric mixer for 4 minutes.

2. Stir in 1 cup walnuts. Pour into prepared pans. Bake 30 to 35 minutes or until toothpick inserted in center comes out clean. Cool in pans 15 minutes. Remove from pans. Cool completely.

3. Combine frosting and remaining ½ teaspoon cinnamon. Stir until blended. Fill and frost cake. Garnish with ¼ cup walnuts.

Makes 12 to 16 servings

Traditional Fruit Cake

3 cups walnut halves
1 (4-ounce) package candied pineapple
1 (8-ounce) package candied cherries
1 (8-ounce) package chopped dates
¾ cup sifted all-purpose flour
¾ cup sugar
½ teaspoon baking powder
½ teaspoon salt
3 eggs, lightly beaten
3 tablespoons dark rum or rum extract
1 tablespoon grated orange peel
1 teaspoon vanilla

1. Preheat oven to 300°F. Line 9×5-inch loaf pan with greased waxed paper.

2. Stir together nuts and fruit in large bowl; set aside.

3. Combine dry ingredients in medium bowl. Sift over nut mixture. Lightly toss dry ingredients and nut mixture together until nut mixture is well coated.

4. Blend in eggs, rum, orange peel and vanilla. Spread into prepared pan.

5. Bake 1 hour and 45 minutes or until golden brown. Cool completely in pan on wire rack before removing cake from pan.

Makes one 9×5-inch loaf

Apple-Cranberry Tart

1⅓ cups all-purpose flour
¾ cup plus 1 tablespoon sugar, divided
¼ teaspoon salt
2 tablespoons vegetable shortening
2 tablespoons margarine
4 to 5 tablespoons ice water
⅓ cup dried cranberries
½ cup boiling water
2 tablespoons cornstarch
1 teaspoon ground cinnamon
4 medium baking apples
Vanilla frozen yogurt (optional)

1. Combine flour, 1 tablespoon sugar and salt in medium bowl. Cut in shortening and margarine with pastry blender or two knives until mixture forms coarse crumbs. Mix in ice water, 1 tablespoon at a time, until mixture comes together and forms a soft dough. Wrap in plastic wrap. Refrigerate 30 minutes.

2. Combine cranberries and boiling water in small bowl. Let stand 20 minutes or until softened.

3. Preheat oven to 425°F. Roll out dough on floured surface to 1/8-inch thickness. Cut into 11-inch circle. If leftover dough remains, reserve scraps to decorate top of tart. Ease dough into 10-inch tart pan with removable bottom leaving 1/4-inch dough above rim of pan. Prick bottom and sides of dough with tines of fork; bake 12 minutes or until dough begins to brown. Cool on wire rack. *Reduce oven temperature to 375°F.*

4. Combine remaining 3/4 cup sugar and cinnamon in large bowl; mix well. Reserve 1 teaspoon mixture for sprinkling over top of tart. Add cornstarch to bowl; mix well. Peel, core and thinly slice apples, adding pieces to bowl as they are sliced; toss well. Drain cranberries; add to apple mixture; toss well.

5. Arrange apple mixture attractively over dough. Sprinkle reserved teaspoon sugar mixture evenly over top of tart. Place tart on baking sheet; bake 30 to 35 minutes or until apples are tender and crust is golden brown. Cool on wire rack. Remove side of pan; place tart on serving plate. Serve warm or at room temperature with frozen yogurt, if desired.

Makes 8 servings

Apple-Cranberry Tart
273

Honey Pumpkin Pie

1 can (16 ounces) solid pack pumpkin
1 cup evaporated low-fat milk
¾ cup honey
3 eggs, slightly beaten
2 tablespoons all-purpose flour
1 teaspoon ground cinnamon
½ teaspoon ground ginger
½ teaspoon rum extract
Pastry for single 9-inch pie crust

Combine all ingredients except pastry in large bowl; beat until well blended. Pour into pastry-lined 9-inch pie plate. Bake at 400°F 45 minutes or until knife inserted near center comes out clean. *Makes 8 servings*

Favorite recipe from National Honey Board

Country Pecan Pie

Pie pastry for single 9-inch pie crust
1¼ cups dark corn syrup
4 eggs
½ cup packed light brown sugar
¼ cup butter or margarine, melted
2 teaspoons all-purpose flour
1½ teaspoons vanilla
1½ cups pecan halves

Preheat oven to 350°F. Roll pastry on lightly floured surface to form 13-inch circle. Fit into 9-inch pie plate. Trim edges; flute. Set aside.

Combine corn syrup, eggs, brown sugar and melted butter in large bowl; beat with electric mixer on medium speed until well blended. Stir in flour and vanilla until blended. Pour into unbaked pie crust. Arrange pecans on top.

Bake 40 to 45 minutes until center of filling is puffed and golden brown. Cool completely on wire rack. Garnish as desired. *Makes one 9-inch pie*

Bûche de Noël

¾ cup cake flour
½ teaspoon baking powder
½ teaspoon salt
5 eggs, separated
1 cup granulated sugar, divided
1 teaspoon vanilla
½ cup powdered sugar
1 cup semisweet chocolate chips
¾ cup heavy cream
1 tablespoon rum
Cocoa Frosting (recipe page 277)
White Chocolate Curls (recipe page 277)
2 teaspoons unsweetened cocoa powder

Preheat oven to 375°F. Grease 15½×10½-inch jelly-roll pan; line pan with waxed paper. Grease waxed paper; set pan aside. Place flour, baking powder and salt in small bowl; stir to combine. Beat egg yolks and ⅔ cup granulated sugar in small bowl with electric mixer at high speed about 5 minutes or until thick and lemon colored, scraping down side of bowl once. Beat in vanilla; set aside.

Beat egg whites in clean large bowl using clean beaters with electric mixer at high speed until foamy. Gradually beat in remaining ⅓ cup granulated sugar, 1 tablespoon at a time, until stiff peaks form.

Fold flour mixture into egg yolk mixture; fold into egg white mixture until evenly incorporated. Spread mixture into prepared pan. Bake 12 to 15 minutes or until cake springs back when lightly touched with finger.

Lightly sift powdered sugar over clean dish towel. Loosen warm cake from edges of pan; invert onto prepared towel. Remove pan; carefully peel off waxed paper. Gently roll up cake in towel from short end, jelly-roll style. Let rolled cake cool completely on wire rack.

For chocolate filling, place chocolate chips and cream in heavy 1-quart saucepan. Heat over low heat until chocolate is melted, stirring frequently. Pour into small bowl; stir in rum. Cover and refrigerate about 1½ hours or until filling is of spreading consistency, stirring occasionally.

Prepare Cocoa Frosting and White Chocolate Curls; refrigerate until ready to use.

Unroll cake; remove towel. Spread cake with chilled chocolate filling to within ½ inch of edge; reroll cake. Spread Cocoa Frosting over cake roll. Garnish with White Chocolate Curls. Sprinkle with cocoa. *Makes 12 servings*

Cocoa Frosting

1 cup heavy cream
2 tablespoons unsweetened Dutch process* cocoa powder, sifted
½ cup powdered sugar, sifted
1 teaspoon vanilla

**The Dutch process, or European-style, cocoa gives this frosting an intense chocolate flavor and a rich color. Other unsweetened cocoas can be substituted, but the flavor may be milder and the color may be lighter.*

Beat cream, cocoa, sugar and vanilla with electric mixer at medium speed until soft peaks form. Do not overbeat. Refrigerate until ready to use. *Makes about 2 cups*

White Chocolate Curls

1 package (8 ounces) white chocolate, coarsely chopped
1 tablespoon vegetable shortening

Place white chocolate and shortening in 2-cup glass measure. Microwave at HIGH about 1½ minutes or until melted, stirring after every 30 seconds. Pour melted white chocolate onto back of baking sheet, marble slab or other heat-resistant flat surface. Quickly spread chocolate into very thin layer with metal spatula. Refrigerate about 10 minutes or until firm, but still pliable. Using small straight-edge metal spatula or paring knife, held at 45° angle, push spatula firmly along baking sheet, under chocolate, so chocolate curls as it is pushed. (If chocolate is too firm to curl, let stand a few minutes at room temperature. Refrigerate again if it becomes too soft.) Using small skewer or toothpick, transfer curls to waxed paper. Store in cool, dry place until ready to use.

Chocolate Hazelnut Torte

1 cup hazelnuts, toasted and skins removed*
¾ cup sugar, divided
¼ cup I CAN'T BELIEVE IT'S NOT BUTTER!® Spread
12 squares (1 ounce each) semi-sweet chocolate, divided
6 large eggs, at room temperature
¼ cup brewed espresso coffee or coffee liqueur
¼ cup whipping or heavy cream, heated to boiling

**Use 1 cup whole blanched almonds, toasted, instead of hazelnuts.*

Preheat oven to 325°F. Grease 9-inch cake pan and line bottom with parchment or waxed paper; set aside.

In food processor or blender, process hazelnuts and ¼ cup sugar until nuts are finely ground; set aside.

In top of double boiler, melt I Can't Believe It's Not Butter! Spread and 10 squares chocolate over medium heat, stirring occasionally, until smooth; set aside and let cool.

In large bowl, with electric mixer, beat eggs and remaining ½ cup sugar until thick and pale yellow, about 4 minutes. Beat in chocolate mixture and espresso. Stir in hazelnut mixture. Pour into prepared pan.

Bake 30 minutes or until toothpick inserted in center comes out with moist crumbs. On wire rack, cool 10 minutes; remove from pan and cool completely.

In small bowl, pour hot cream over remaining 2 squares chocolate, chopped. Stir until chocolate is melted and mixture is smooth. Pour chocolate mixture over torte to glaze. Let stand at room temperature or refrigerate until chocolate mixture is set, about 30 minutes.

Makes 8 servings

Note: Torte may be frozen up to 1 month.

Cranberry Apple Pie with Soft Gingersnap Crust

20 gingersnaps
1½ tablespoons margarine
2 McIntosh apples
1 cup fresh cranberries
5 tablespoons dark brown sugar
¼ teaspoon ground cinnamon
¼ teaspoon vanilla
1 teaspoon granulated sugar

Preheat oven to 375°F. Combine gingersnaps and margarine in food processor; process until well combined. Press gingersnap mixture into 8-inch pie plate. Press on crust with slightly smaller pie plate to make crust even. Bake 5 to 8 minutes; remove crust from oven and let cool. Slice apples in food processor. Add cranberries, brown sugar, cinnamon and vanilla; stir just until mixed. Spoon mixture into separate pie plate or casserole dish; sprinkle with granulated sugar. Bake 35 minutes or until tender. Spoon over gingersnap crust and serve immediately. *Makes 8 servings*

Favorite recipe from The Sugar Association, Inc.

Cranberry Apple Pie with Soft Gingersnap Crust

Decadent Triple Layer Mud Pie

¼ cup sweetened condensed milk
2 (1-ounce) squares semi-sweet baking chocolate, melted
1 (6-ounce) READY CRUST® Chocolate Pie Crust
¾ cup chopped pecans, toasted
2 cups cold milk
2 (4-serving-size) packages JELL-O® Chocolate Flavor Instant Pudding & Pie Filling
1 (8-ounce) tub COOL WHIP® Whipped Topping, thawed, divided

1. Combine sweetened condensed milk and chocolate in medium bowl; stir until smooth. Pour into crust. Press nuts evenly onto chocolate mixture in crust. Refrigerate 10 minutes.

2. Pour milk into large bowl. Add pudding mixes. Beat with wire whisk 2 minutes or until smooth. (Mixture will be thick.) Spread 1½ cups pudding over chocolate mixture in crust. Immediately stir half of whipped topping into remaining pudding. Spread over pudding in crust. Top with remaining whipped topping.

3. Refrigerate 3 hours or until set. Garnish as desired. Refrigerate leftovers.

Makes 8 servings

Prep Time: 10 minutes
Chill Time: 3 hours

Ginger-Crusted Pumpkin Cheesecake

12 whole low-fat honey graham crackers, broken into small pieces
3 tablespoons reduced-fat margarine, melted
½ teaspoon ground ginger
1 can (15 ounces) solid-pack pumpkin
2 packages (8 ounces each) fat-free cream cheese, softened
1 package (8 ounces) reduced-fat cream cheese, softened
1 cup sugar
1 cup cholesterol-free egg substitute
½ cup nonfat evaporated milk
1 tablespoon vanilla
1 teaspoon ground cinnamon
½ teaspoon ground nutmeg
¼ teaspoon salt
2 cups thawed frozen reduced-fat whipped topping
Additional ground nutmeg (optional)

1. Preheat oven to 350°F. Coat 9-inch springform baking pan with nonstick cooking spray; set aside.

2. Place graham crackers, margarine and ginger in food processor or blender; pulse until coarse in texture. Gently press crumb mixture onto bottom and ¾ inch up side of pan. Bake 10 minutes or until lightly browned; cool slightly on wire rack.

3. Beat remaining ingredients except whipped topping and additional nutmeg in large bowl with electric mixer at medium-high speed until smooth; pour into pie crust.

4. Bake 1 hour and 15 minutes or until top begins to crack and center moves very little when pan is shaken back and forth. Cool on wire rack to room temperature; refrigerate until ready to serve.

5. Just before serving, spoon 1 tablespoon whipped topping on each serving; sprinkle lightly with additional nutmeg.

Makes 16 servings

Cook's Tip: This cheesecake freezes well. In fact, the flavors improve if frozen!

White Chocolate Cranberry Tart

1 refrigerated pie crust (half of 15-ounce package)
1 cup sugar
2 eggs
¼ cup butter, melted
2 teaspoons vanilla
½ cup all-purpose flour
1 package (6 ounces) white chocolate baking bar, chopped
½ cup chopped macadamia nuts, lightly toasted*
½ cup dried cranberries, coarsely chopped

**Toast chopped macadamia nuts in hot skillet about 3 minutes or until fragrant.*

1. Preheat oven to 350°F. Line 9-inch tart pan with removable bottom or pie pan with pie crust (refrigerate or freeze other crust for another use).

2. Combine sugar, eggs, butter and vanilla in large bowl; mix well. Stir in flour until well blended. Add white chocolate, nuts and cranberries.

3. Pour filling into unbaked crust. Bake 50 to 55 minutes or until top of tart is crusty and deep golden brown and knife inserted in center comes out clean.

4. Cool completely on wire rack. Cover and store at room temperature until serving time.

Makes 8 servings

Serve it with Style!: Top each serving with a dollop of whipped cream flavored with ground cinnamon, a favorite liqueur and grated orange peel.

Make-Ahead Time: Up to 2 days before serving

Maple Pumpkin Cheesecake

1¼ cups graham cracker crumbs
¼ cup sugar
¼ cup (½ stick) butter or margarine, melted
3 (8-ounce) packages cream cheese, softened
1 (14-ounce) can EAGLE® BRAND Sweetened Condensed Milk (NOT evaporated milk)
1 (15-ounce) can pumpkin
3 eggs
¼ cup maple syrup
1½ teaspoons ground cinnamon
1 teaspoon ground nutmeg
½ teaspoon salt
Maple Pecan Glaze (recipe follows)

1. Preheat oven to 325°F. In small mixing bowl, combine crumbs, sugar and butter; press firmly on bottom of 9-inch springform pan.* In large mixing bowl, beat cream cheese until fluffy. Gradually beat in Eagle Brand until smooth. Add pumpkin, eggs, maple syrup, cinnamon, nutmeg and salt; mix well. Pour into prepared pan. Bake 1¼ hours or until center appears nearly set when shaken. Cool 1 hour. Cover and chill at least 4 hours.

2. To serve, spoon some Maple Pecan Glaze over cheesecake. Garnish with whipped cream and pecans, if desired. Pass remaining sauce. Store leftovers covered in refrigerator.

Makes one 9-inch cheesecake

**To use 13×9-inch baking pan, press crumb mixture firmly on bottom of pan. Proceed as directed, except bake 50 to 60 minutes or until center appears nearly set when shaken.*

Maple Pecan Glaze: In medium saucepan over medium-high heat, combine ¾ cup maple syrup and 1 cup (½ pint) whipping cream; bring to a boil. Boil rapidly 15 to 20 minutes or until thickened, stirring occasionally. Add ½ cup chopped pecans.

Prep Time: 25 minutes
Bake Time: 1 hour and 15 minutes
Cool Time: 1 hour
Chill Time: 4 hours

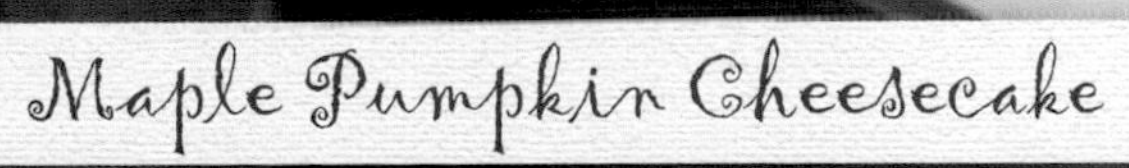
Maple Pumpkin Cheesecake

Apple Cider Cake

1 recipe Marzipan (recipe follows)
Red, yellow and green food colors
1 package (2-layer size) spice cake mix
1¼ cups apple cider
⅓ cup vegetable oil
3 eggs
Apple Cider Filling (recipe page 293)
Apple Cider Frosting (recipe page 293)
2 cups coarsely chopped walnuts
Whole cloves

1. Prepare Marzipan. Divide into thirds; place each part in separate small bowl. Color 1 part with red food color, second part with yellow food color and remaining part with green food color; cover and set aside.

2. Preheat oven to 350°F. Grease and flour two 9-inch round baking pans.

3. Combine cake mix, apple cider, oil and eggs in medium bowl. Beat at low speed of electric mixer until blended; beat at medium speed 2 minutes. Pour batter evenly into prepared pans.

4. Bake 30 to 35 minutes until wooden toothpick inserted into centers comes out clean. Let cool in pans on wire racks 10 minutes. Remove to racks; cool completely.

5. Prepare Apple Cider Filling and Apple Cider Frosting. Place 1 cake layer on serving plate; top with Apple Cider Filling. Top with second cake layer; frost top and side of cake with Apple Cider Frosting. Press nuts onto side of cake.

6. Form red and yellow Marzipan into apple shapes. Place cloves in tops of apples for stems. Roll out green Marzipan to ¼-inch thickness; cut out leaf shapes as desired. Arrange on top and around side of cake.

Makes 12 servings

Marzipan

1 can (8 ounces) almond paste
1 egg white*
3 cups powdered sugar

**Use only grade A clean, uncracked egg.*

Combine almond paste and egg white in small bowl. Add 2 cups powdered sugar; mix well. Knead in remaining 1 cup sugar until smooth and pliable. Wrap tightly in plastic wrap; refrigerate until ready to serve.

Makes about 2 cups

Apple Cider Filling

⅓ cup sugar
3 tablespoons cornstarch
⅔ cup apple cider
½ cup apple butter
2 tablespoons lemon juice
2 tablespoons butter or margarine

Combine sugar and cornstarch in small saucepan. Stir in cider and apple butter; cook over medium heat, stirring constantly, until thickened. Remove from heat; stir in lemon juice and butter. Cool completely. *Makes about 1¼ cups*

Apple Cider Frosting

½ cup butter or margarine, softened
¼ cup apple cider
4 cups (about 1 pound) powdered sugar

In medium bowl, beat butter and cider until creamy and well blended. Gradually beat in powdered sugar until smooth. *Makes about 4 cups*

Holiday Cheese Tarts

1 (8-ounce) package cream cheese, softened
1 (14-ounce) can EAGLE® BRAND Sweetened Condensed Milk (NOT evaporated milk)
⅓ cup lemon juice from concentrate
1 teaspoon vanilla extract
2 (4-ounce) packages single-serve graham cracker crumb pie crusts
Assorted fruit (strawberries, blueberries, bananas, raspberries, orange segments, cherries, kiwi fruit, grapes, pineapple, etc.)
¼ cup apple jelly, melted, if desired

1. In medium mixing bowl, beat cream cheese until fluffy. Gradually beat in Eagle Brand until smooth. Stir in lemon juice and vanilla.

2. Spoon into crusts. Chill 2 hours or until set. Just before serving, top with fruit; brush with jelly, if desired. Refrigerate leftovers. *Makes 12 tarts*

Prep Time: 10 minutes
Chill Time: 2 hours

Double Layer Pumpkin Pie

4 ounces cream cheese, softened
1 cup plus 1 tablespoon milk or half-and-half, divided
1 tablespoon sugar
1½ cups thawed frozen whipped topping, plus additional for garnish
1 (6-ounce) READY CRUST® Graham Cracker Pie Crust
2 (4-serving-size) packages vanilla flavor instant pudding & pie filling
2 teaspoons pumpkin pie spice*
1 (16-ounce) can pumpkin

**May substitute with 1 teaspoon ground cinnamon, ½ teaspoon ground ginger and ¼ teaspoon ground cloves*

1. Mix cream cheese, 1 tablespoon milk and sugar in large bowl with wire whisk until smooth. Gently stir in whipped topping. Spread on bottom of crust.

2. Pour 1 cup milk into bowl. Add pudding mixes. Beat with wire whisk 1 minute. (Mixture will be thick.) Stir in pumpkin and spices with wire whisk until well blended. Spread over cream cheese layer.

3. Refrigerate 4 hours or until set. Garnish with additional whipped topping, if desired. Refrigerate leftovers. *Makes 8 servings*

Prep Time: 10 minutes
Chill Time: 4 hours

Ribbon of Cherry Cheesecake

1 cup sliced almonds, toasted and finely chopped
1 cup graham cracker crumbs
⅓ cup butter or margarine, melted
1 (21-ounce) can cherry pie filling
¾ cup plus 2 tablespoons sugar, divided
2 tablespoons cornstarch
½ teaspoon almond extract
4 (8-ounce each) packages cream cheese, softened
3 tablespoons amaretto liqueur
1 tablespoon lemon juice
1 teaspoon vanilla extract
3 eggs, lightly beaten

Combine almonds, graham cracker crumbs and butter in medium bowl; mix well. Press crumb mixture evenly over the bottom and 2 inches up side of 10-inch springform pan. Set aside.

Purée cherry pie filling in blender or food processor until smooth; pour into medium saucepan. Combine 2 tablespoons sugar and cornstarch; stir into cherry filling. Cook, stirring constantly, over low heat until mixture is thick and bubbly. Remove from heat. Stir in almond extract. Set aside to cool.

Combine cream cheese, remaining ¾ cup sugar, amaretto, lemon juice and vanilla in large mixing bowl. Beat with electric mixer on medium speed 3 to 4 minutes, or until well mixed. Add eggs all at once; beat on low speed just until mixed.

To assemble cheesecake, pour one-third of the cream cheese mixture into prepared crust. Top with about ⅓ cup cherry purée. Swirl cherry mixture into cream cheese mixture, using knife or spatula. Repeat layers twice, ending with cherry purée. Reserve remaining purée.

Bake in preheated 350°F oven 60 to 65 minutes, or until center appears nearly set when gently shaken. Cool on wire rack. Refrigerate until ready to serve. To serve, spoon generous tablespoons of purée on serving plate. Place cheesecake wedge on top of purée.

Makes 16 servings

Favorite recipe from Cherry Marketing Institute

Peppermint Cake

Cake

2¼ cups cake flour
2 teaspoons baking powder
1 teaspoon salt
½ teaspoon baking soda
1½ cups sugar
2 tablespoons margarine, softened
½ cup MOTT'S® Natural Apple Sauce
½ cup skim milk
4 egg whites
1 teaspoon vanilla extract

Peppermint Frosting

1½ cups sugar
¼ cup water
2 egg whites
¼ teaspoon cream of tartar
½ teaspoon peppermint extract
3 tablespoons crushed starlight candies (about 6)

1. Preheat oven to 350°F. Spray 9-inch round cake pan with nonstick cooking spray.

2. To prepare Cake, in medium bowl, combine flour, baking powder, salt and baking soda. In large bowl, beat 1½ cups sugar and margarine with electric mixer at medium speed until blended. Whisk in apple sauce, milk, 4 egg whites and vanilla.

3. Add flour mixture to apple sauce mixture; stir until well blended. Pour batter into prepared pan.

4. Bake 35 to 40 minutes or until toothpick inserted in center comes out clean. Cool completely on wire rack. Split cake horizontally in half to make 2 layers.

5. To prepare Peppermint Frosting, in top of double boiler, whisk together 1½ cups sugar, water, 2 egg whites and cream of tartar. Cook, whisking occasionally, over simmering water 4 minutes or until mixture is hot and sugar is dissolved. Remove from heat; stir in peppermint extract. Beat with electric mixer at high speed 3 minutes or until mixture forms stiff peaks.

6. Place one cake layer on serving plate. Spread with layer of Peppermint Frosting. Top with second cake layer. Frost top and side with remaining Peppermint Frosting. Sprinkle top and side of cake with crushed candies. Cut into 12 slices. Refrigerate leftovers.

Makes 12 servings

Celebration Pumpkin Cake

1 package (18 ounces) spice cake mix
1 can (16 ounces) pumpkin
3 eggs
¼ cup butter, softened
1½ containers (16 ounces each) cream cheese frosting
⅓ cup caramel topping
Pecan halves for garnish

Preheat oven to 350°F. Grease and flour 3 (9-inch) round cake pans. Combine cake mix, pumpkin, eggs and butter in large bowl; beat with electric mixer at medium speed 2 minutes. Divide batter evenly among prepared pans. Bake 20 to 25 minutes or until toothpick inserted in centers comes out clean. Cool 5 minutes on wire rack; remove from pans and cool completely.

Place one cake layer on serving plate; cover with frosting. Repeat layers, ending with frosting. Frost side of cake. Spread caramel topping over top of cake, letting some caramel drip down side. Garnish with pecan halves. *Makes 16 servings*

Cranberry Walnut Cheesecake

1¼ cups cold milk
2 (4-serving-size) packages JELL-O® Cheesecake Flavor Instant Pudding & Pie Filling
½ teaspoon grated lemon peel
1 (8-ounce) tub COOL WHIP® Whipped Topping, thawed, divided
1 (6-ounce) READY CRUST® Graham Cracker Pie Crust
1 (16-ounce) can whole berry cranberry sauce, divided
½ cup toasted chopped walnuts, divided

1. Pour milk into large bowl. Add pudding mixes and lemon peel. Beat with wire whisk 1 minute. Gently stir in half of whipped topping. Spread half of pudding mixture on bottom of crust.

2. Spread half of cranberry sauce over pudding mixture. Sprinkle with ¼ cup walnuts. Top with remaining pudding mixture.

3. Refrigerate 4 hours until set. Garnish with remaining whipped topping and ¼ cup walnuts. Serve with remaining cranberry sauce. Refrigerate leftovers.

Makes 10 servings

Prep Time: 15 minutes
Chill Time: 4 hours

Cranberry Apple Nut Pie

Rich Pie Pastry (recipe follows)
1 cup sugar
3 tablespoons all-purpose flour
¼ teaspoon salt
4 cups sliced peeled tart apples (4 large apples)
2 cups fresh cranberries
½ cup golden raisins
½ cup coarsely chopped pecans
1 tablespoon grated lemon peel
2 tablespoons butter
1 egg, beaten

Preheat oven to 425°F. Divide pie pastry in half. Roll one half on lightly floured surface to form 13-inch circle. Fit into 9-inch pie plate; trim edges. Reroll scraps and cut into decorative shapes, such as holly leaves and berries, for garnish; set aside.

Combine sugar, flour and salt in large bowl. Stir in apples, cranberries, raisins, pecans and lemon peel; toss well. Spoon fruit mixture into unbaked pie crust. Dot with butter. Roll remaining half of pie pastry on lightly floured surface to form 11-inch circle. Place over filling. Trim and seal edges; flute. Cut 3 slits in center of top crust. Moisten pastry cutouts and use to decorate top crust as desired. Lightly brush top crust with egg.

Bake 35 to 40 minutes or until apples are tender when pierced with fork and pastry is golden brown. Cool in pan on wire rack. Serve warm or cool completely.

Makes 1 (9-inch) pie

Rich Pie Pastry

2 cups all-purpose flour
¼ teaspoon salt
6 tablespoons cold butter
6 tablespoons shortening or lard
6 to 8 tablespoons cold water

Combine flour and salt in medium bowl. Cut in butter and lard with pastry blender or 2 knives until mixture resembles coarse crumbs. Sprinkle water, 1 tablespoon at a time, over flour mixture, mixing until flour is moistened. Shape dough into a ball. Roll, fill and bake as recipe directs. *Makes pastry for 1 (9-inch) double pie crust*

Note: For single crust, cut recipe in half.

Fudgy Pecan Pie

¼ cup (½ stick) butter or margarine
2 (1-ounce) squares unsweetened chocolate
1 (14-ounce) can EAGLE® BRAND Sweetened Condensed Milk (NOT evaporated milk)
½ cup hot water
2 eggs, well beaten
1¼ cups pecan halves or pieces
1 teaspoon vanilla extract
⅛ teaspoon salt
1 (9-inch) unbaked pastry shell

1. Preheat oven to 350°F. In medium saucepan over low heat, melt butter and chocolate. Stir in Eagle Brand, hot water and eggs; mix well.

2. Remove from heat; stir in pecans, vanilla and salt. Pour into pastry shell. Bake 40 to 45 minutes or until center is set. Cool slightly. Serve warm or chilled. Garnish as desired. Store covered in refrigerator. *Makes 1 (9-inch) pie*

Prep Time: 15 minutes
Bake Time: 40 to 45 minutes

Holiday Peppermint Slices

1 package (18 ounces) refrigerated sugar cookie dough
¼ teaspoon peppermint extract, divided
Red food coloring
Green food coloring

1. Remove dough from wrapper according to package directions. Cut dough into thirds.

2. Combine ⅓ of dough, ⅛ teaspoon peppermint extract and enough red food coloring to make dough desired shade of red. Knead dough until evenly tinted.

3. Repeat with second ⅓ of dough, remaining ⅛ teaspoon peppermint extract and green food coloring.

4. To assemble, shape each portion of dough into 8-inch roll. Place red roll beside green roll; press together slightly. Place plain roll on top. Press rolls together to form one tri-colored roll; wrap in plastic wrap. Refrigerate 2 hours or overnight.

5. Preheat oven to 350°F.

6. Cut dough into ¼-inch-thick slices. Place 2 inches apart on ungreased cookie sheets. Bake 8 to 9 minutes or until set but not browned. Cool 1 minute on cookie sheets. Cool completely on wire racks.

Makes 2½ dozen cookies

Homemade Coconut Macaroons

3 egg whites
¼ teaspoon cream of tartar
⅛ teaspoon salt
¾ cup sugar
2¼ cups shredded coconut, toasted*
1 teaspoon vanilla

**To toast coconut, spread evenly on cookie sheet. Toast in preheated 350°F oven 7 minutes. Stir and toast 1 to 2 minutes more or until light golden brown.*

Preheat oven to 325°F. Line cookie sheets with parchment paper or foil. Beat egg whites, cream of tartar and salt in large bowl with electric mixer until soft peaks form. Beat in sugar, 1 tablespoon at a time, until egg whites are stiff and shiny. Fold in coconut and vanilla. Drop tablespoonfuls of dough 4 inches apart onto prepared cookie sheets; spread each into 3-inch circles with back of spoon.

Bake 18 to 22 minutes or until light brown. Cool 1 minute on cookie sheets. Remove to wire racks; cool completely. Store in airtight container. *Makes about 2 dozen cookies*

Honey Spice Balls

½ cup butter, softened
½ cup packed brown sugar
1 egg
1 tablespoon honey
1 teaspoon vanilla extract
2 cups all-purpose flour
½ teaspoon baking powder
½ teaspoon ground cinnamon
¼ teaspoon ground nutmeg
Uncooked quick oats

Preheat oven to 350°F. Grease cookie sheets. Beat butter and brown sugar in large bowl with electric mixer until creamy. Add egg, honey and vanilla; beat until light and fluffy. Stir in flour, baking powder, cinnamon and nutmeg until well blended. Shape tablespoonfuls of dough into balls; roll in oats. Place 2 inches apart on prepared cookie sheets.

Bake 15 to 18 minutes until cookie tops crack slightly. Cool 1 minute on cookie sheets. Remove to wire racks; cool completely. Store in airtight container.

Makes about 2½ dozen cookies

Left to right: Homemade Coconut Macaroons and Honey Spice Balls

Buttery Almond Cutouts

1 cup butter, softened
1½ cups granulated sugar
¾ cup sour cream
2 eggs
3 teaspoons almond extract, divided
1 teaspoon vanilla
4⅓ cups all-purpose flour
1 teaspoon baking powder
1 teaspoon baking soda
½ teaspoon salt
2 cups powdered sugar
2 tablespoons milk
1 tablespoon light corn syrup
Assorted food colorings

1. Beat butter and granulated sugar in large bowl until light and fluffy. Add sour cream, eggs, 2 teaspoons almond extract and vanilla; beat until smooth. Add flour, baking powder, baking soda and salt; beat just until well blended.

2. Divide dough into 4 pieces; flatten each piece into a disc. Wrap each disc tightly with plastic wrap. Refrigerate at least 3 hours or up to 3 days.

3. Combine powdered sugar, milk, corn syrup and remaining 1 teaspoon almond extract in small bowl; stir until smooth. Cover and refrigerate up to 3 days.

4. Preheat oven to 375°F. Working with 1 disc of dough at a time, roll out on floured surface to ¼-inch thickness. Cut dough into desired shapes using 2½-inch cookie cutters. Place about 2 inches apart on ungreased baking sheets. Bake 7 to 8 minutes or until edges are firm and bottoms are brown. Remove from baking sheets to wire racks to cool.

5. Separate powdered sugar mixture into 3 or 4 batches in small bowls; tint each batch with desired food coloring. Frost cookies.

Makes about 3 dozen cookies

Note: To freeze dough, place wrapped discs in resealable plastic food storage bags. Thaw at room temperature before using. Or, cut out dough, bake and cool cookies completely. Freeze unglazed cookies for up to 2 months. Thaw and glaze as desired.

Make-Ahead Time: Up to 3 days in refrigerator or up to 3 months in freezer
Final Prep Time: 30 minutes

Chocolate Almond Biscotti

1 package DUNCAN HINES® Moist Deluxe® Dark Chocolate Cake Mix
1 cup all-purpose flour
½ cup butter or margarine, melted
2 eggs
1 teaspoon almond extract
½ cup chopped almonds
White chocolate, melted (optional)

1. Preheat oven to 350°F. Line 2 baking sheets with parchment paper.

2. Combine cake mix, flour, butter, eggs and almond extract in large bowl. Beat at low speed with electric mixer until well blended; stir in almonds. Divide dough in half. Shape each half into 12×2-inch log; place logs on prepared baking sheets. (Bake logs separately.)

3. Bake at 350°F for 30 to 35 minutes or until toothpick inserted in centers comes out clean. Remove logs from oven; cool on baking sheets 15 minutes. Using serrated knife, cut logs into ½-inch slices. Arrange slices on baking sheets. Bake biscotti 10 minutes. Remove to cooling racks; cool completely.

4. Dip one end of each biscotti in melted white chocolate, if desired. Allow white chocolate to set at room temperature before storing biscotti in airtight container.

Makes about 2½ dozen cookies

Molasses Spice Cookies

- 1 cup granulated sugar
- ¾ cup shortening
- ¼ cup molasses
- 1 egg, beaten
- 2 cups all-purpose flour
- 2 teaspoons baking soda
- 1 teaspoon ground cinnamon
- 1 teaspoon ground cloves
- 1 teaspoon ground ginger
- ¼ teaspoon dry mustard
- ¼ teaspoon salt
- ½ cup granulated brown sugar or granulated sugar

1. Preheat oven to 375°F. Grease cookie sheets; set aside.

2. Beat granulated sugar and shortening about 5 minutes in large bowl until light and fluffy. Add molasses and egg; beat until fluffy.

3. Combine flour, baking soda, cinnamon, cloves, ginger, mustard and salt in medium bowl. Add to shortening mixture; mix until just combined.

4. Place brown sugar in shallow dish. Roll tablespoonfuls of dough into 1-inch balls; roll in sugar to coat. Place 2 inches apart on prepared cookie sheets. Bake 15 minutes or until lightly browned. Let cookies stand on cookie sheets 2 minutes. Remove cookies to wire racks; cool completely.

Makes about 6 dozen cookies

Helpful Hint: Looking for something different to take to all your holiday gatherings? Decorate a metal tin with rubber stamps for a crafty look and fill it with Molasses Spice Cookies and an assortment of uniquely flavored teas. Perfect for a twist on your traditional hostess gift.

Almond-Orange Shortbread

1 cup (4 ounces) sliced almonds, divided
2 cups all-purpose flour
1 cup cold butter, cut into pieces
½ cup sugar
½ cup cornstarch
2 tablespoons grated orange peel
1 teaspoon almond extract

1. Preheat oven to 350°F. To toast almonds, spread ¾ cup almonds in single layer in large baking pan. Bake 6 minutes or until golden brown, stirring frequently. Remove almonds from oven. Cool completely in pan. *Reduce oven temperature to 325°F.*

2. Place toasted almonds in food processor. Process using on/off pulsing action until almonds are coarsely chopped.

3. Add flour, butter, sugar, cornstarch, orange peel and almond extract to food processor. Process using on/off pulsing action until mixture resembles coarse crumbs.

4. Press dough firmly and evenly into 10×8½-inch rectangle on large ungreased cookie sheet with fingers. Score dough into 1¼-inch squares with knife. Press one slice of remaining almonds in center of each square.

5. Bake 30 to 40 minutes or until shortbread is firm when pressed and lightly browned.

6. Immediately cut into squares along score lines with sharp knife. Remove cookies with spatula to wire racks; cool completely.

7. Store loosely covered at room temperature up to 1 week.

Makes about 5 dozen cookies

Elephant Ears

1 package (17¼ ounces) frozen puff pastry, thawed according to package directions
1 egg, beaten
¼ cup sugar, divided
2 squares (1 ounce each) semisweet chocolate

Preheat oven to 375°F. Grease cookie sheets; sprinkle lightly with water. Roll one sheet of pastry to 12×10-inch rectangle. Brush with egg; sprinkle with 1 tablespoon sugar. Tightly roll up 10-inch sides, meeting in center. Brush center with egg and seal rolls tightly together; turn over. Cut into ⅜-inch-thick slices. Place slices on prepared cookie sheets. Sprinkle with 1 tablespoon sugar. Repeat with remaining pastry, egg and sugar. Bake 16 to 18 minutes until golden brown. Remove to wire racks; cool completely.

Melt chocolate in small saucepan over low heat, stirring constantly. Remove from heat. Spread bottoms of cookies with chocolate. Place on wire rack, chocolate side up. Let stand until chocolate is set. Store between layers of waxed paper in airtight containers.

Makes about 4 dozen cookies

Chocolate Raspberry Thumbprints

1½ cups butter, softened
1 cup sugar
1 egg
1 teaspoon vanilla extract
3 cups all-purpose flour
¼ cup unsweetened cocoa powder
½ teaspoon salt
1 cup (6 ounces) semisweet mini chocolate chips
⅔ cup raspberry preserves
Powdered sugar (optional)

Preheat oven to 350°F. Grease cookie sheets. Beat butter and sugar in large bowl. Beat in egg and vanilla until light and fluffy. Mix in flour, cocoa and salt until well blended. Stir in chocolate chips. Roll level tablespoonfuls of dough into balls. Place 2 inches apart on prepared cookie sheets. Make deep indentation in center of each ball with thumb.

Bake 12 to 15 minutes until just set. Cool 2 minutes on cookie sheets. Remove to wire racks; cool completely. Fill centers with raspberry preserves and sprinkle with powdered sugar, if desired. Store between layers of waxed paper in airtight containers.

Makes about 4½ dozen cookies

Top to bottom: Elephant Ears and Chocolate Raspberry Thumbprints

Chocolate Madeleines

3 teaspoons butter, softened, divided
1¼ cups cake flour or all-purpose flour
¼ cup unsweetened cocoa powder
¼ teaspoon salt
¼ teaspoon baking powder
1 cup granulated sugar
2 eggs
¾ cup butter, melted and cooled
2 tablespoons almond-flavored liqueur or kirsch
Powdered sugar

1. Preheat oven to 375°F. Grease 3 madeleine pans with softened butter, 1 teaspoon per pan; dust with flour; set aside.

2. Place flour, cocoa, salt and baking powder in medium bowl; stir to combine.

3. Beat sugar and eggs in large bowl with electric mixer at medium speed 5 minutes or until mixture is light in color, thick and falls in wide ribbons from beaters. Beat in flour mixture at low speed until well blended. Beat in melted butter and liqueur until just blended.

4. Spoon level tablespoonfuls of batter into each prepared madeleine mold. Bake 12 minutes or until puffed and golden brown.

5. Let madeleines stand in pan 1 minute. Carefully loosen cookies from pan with point of small knife. Invert pan over wire rack; tap lightly to release cookies. Cool completely. (Cookies should be shell side up.)

6. Dust with sifted powdered sugar. Store tightly covered at room temperature up to 24 hours or freeze up to 3 months. *Makes about 3 dozen madeleines*

Note: If only 1 madeleine pan is available, thoroughly wash, dry, regrease and flour after baking each batch. Cover remaining dough with plastic wrap and let stand at room temperature.

Chocolate Madeleines

Christmas Tree Platter

1 recipe Christmas Ornament Cookie Dough (recipe follows)
2 cups sifted powdered sugar
2 tablespoons milk or lemon juice
Assorted food colors, colored sugars and assorted small decors

1. Preheat oven to 350°F. Prepare Christmas Ornament Cookie Dough. Divide dough in half. Reserve 1 half; refrigerate remaining dough. Roll reserved half of dough to 1/8-inch thickness.

2. Cut out tree shapes with cookie cutters. Place on ungreased cookie sheets.

3. Bake 10 to 12 minutes or until edges are lightly browned. Remove to wire racks; cool completely.

4. Repeat with remaining half of dough. Reroll scraps; cut into small circles for ornaments, squares and rectangles for gift boxes and tree trunks.

5. Bake 8 to 12 minutes, depending on size of cookies.

6. Mix sugar and milk for icing. Tint most of icing green and a smaller amount red or other colors for ornaments and boxes. Spread green icing on trees. Sprinkle ornaments and boxes with colored sugars or decorate as desired. Arrange cookies on flat platter to resemble tree as shown in photo. *Makes about 1 dozen cookies*

Tip: Use this beautiful Christmas Tree Platter cookie as your centerpiece for this holiday family dinner. It's sure to receive lots of "oohs" and "ahs"!

Christmas Ornament Cookie Dough

2¼ cups all-purpose flour
¼ teaspoon salt
1 cup sugar
¾ cup butter, softened
1 egg
1 teaspoon vanilla
1 teaspoon almond extract

1. Combine flour and salt in medium bowl.

2. Beat sugar and butter in large bowl at medium speed of electric mixer until fluffy. Beat in egg, vanilla and almond extract. Gradually add flour mixture. Beat at low speed until well blended.

3. Form dough into 2 discs; wrap in plastic wrap and refrigerate 30 minutes or until firm.

Chocolate-Pecan Angels

1 cup mini semisweet chocolate chips
1 cup chopped pecans, toasted
1 cup sifted powdered sugar
1 egg white

Preheat oven to 350°F. Grease cookie sheets. Combine chips, pecans and powdered sugar in medium bowl. Add egg white; mix well. Drop batter by teaspoonfuls 2 inches apart onto prepared cookie sheets.

Bake 11 to 12 minutes or until edges are light golden brown. Let cookies stand on cookie sheets 1 minute. Remove cookies to wire racks; cool completely.

Makes about 3 dozen cookies

Chocolate Chip Cranberry Cheese Bars

1 cup (2 sticks) butter or margarine, softened
1 cup packed brown sugar
2 cups all-purpose flour
1½ cups quick or old-fashioned oats
2 teaspoons grated orange peel
2 cups (12-ounce package) NESTLÉ® TOLL HOUSE® Semi-Sweet Chocolate Morsels
1 cup (4 ounces) sweetened dried cranberries
1 package (8 ounces) cream cheese, softened
1 can (14 ounces) NESTLÉ® CARNATION® Sweetened Condensed Milk

PREHEAT oven to 350°F. Grease 13×9-inch baking pan.

BEAT butter and sugar in large mixer bowl until creamy. Gradually beat in flour, oats and orange peel until crumbly. Stir in morsels and cranberries; reserve *2 cups* mixture. Press *remaining* mixture onto bottom of prepared baking pan.

BAKE for 15 minutes. Beat cream cheese in small mixer bowl until smooth. Gradually beat in sweetened condensed milk. Pour over hot crust; sprinkle with reserved mixture. Bake for 25 to 30 minutes or until center is set. Cool in pan on wire rack. Cut into bars.

Makes about 3 dozen bars

Autumn Apple Bars

Crust

Milk
1 egg yolk (reserve egg white)
2½ cups all-purpose flour
1 teaspoon salt
1 cup butter, softened

Filling

1 cup graham cracker crumbs
8 cups tart cooking apples, peeled, cored and sliced to ¼-inch thickness (about 8 to 10 medium)
1 cup plus 2 tablespoons granulated sugar, divided
2½ teaspoons ground cinnamon, divided
¼ teaspoon ground nutmeg
1 egg white
1 teaspoon ground cinnamon

Drizzle

1 cup powdered sugar
1 to 2 tablespoons milk
½ teaspoon vanilla

1. Preheat oven to 350°F. For crust, add enough milk to egg yolk to measure ⅔ cup; set aside. Combine flour and salt in medium bowl. Cut in butter until crumbly using pastry blender or two knives. With fork, stir in milk mixture until dough forms ball; divide into 2 halves. Roll out ½ to 15×10-inch rectangle on lightly floured surface. Place on bottom of ungreased 15×10×1-inch jelly-roll pan.

2. For filling, sprinkle graham cracker crumbs over top of dough; layer apple slices over crumbs. Combine 1 cup granulated sugar, 1½ teaspoons cinnamon and nutmeg in small bowl; sprinkle over apples.

3. Roll out remaining dough into 15×10½-inch rectangle; place over apples. With fork, beat egg white in small bowl until foamy; brush over top crust. Stir together remaining 2 tablespoons granulated sugar and remaining 1 teaspoon cinnamon in another small bowl; sprinkle over crust. Bake 45 to 60 minutes or until lightly browned.

4. For drizzle, stir together all ingredients in small bowl. Drizzle over top; cut into bars.

Makes about 3 dozen bars

Icicle Ornaments

2½ cups all-purpose flour
¼ teaspoon salt
1 cup sugar
¾ cup unsalted butter, softened
2 squares (1 ounce each) white chocolate, melted
1 egg
1 teaspoon vanilla
Coarse white decorating sugar, colored sugars and decors
Ribbon

1. Combine flour and salt in medium bowl. Beat sugar and butter in large bowl at medium speed of electric mixer until fluffy. Beat in melted white chocolate, egg and vanilla. Gradually add flour mixture. Beat at low speed until well blended. Shape dough into disc. Wrap in plastic wrap and refrigerate 30 minutes or until firm.

2. Preheat oven to 350°F. Grease cookie sheets. Shape heaping tablespoonfuls of dough into 10-inch ropes. Fold each rope in half; twist to make icicle shape, leaving opening at top and tapering ends. Roll in coarse sugar; sprinkle with colored sugars and decors as desired. Place 1 inch apart on prepared cookie sheets.

3. Bake 8 to 10 minutes. (Do not brown.) Cool on cookie sheets 1 minute. Remove to wire racks; cool completely. Pull ribbon through opening in top of each icicle; tie small knot in ribbon ends.

Makes about 2½ dozen cookies

Orange-Almond Sables

1½ cups powdered sugar
1 cup butter, softened
1 tablespoon finely grated orange peel
1 tablespoon almond-flavored liqueur *or* 1 teaspoon almond extract
¾ cup whole blanched almonds, toasted*
1¾ cups all-purpose flour
¼ teaspoon salt
1 egg, beaten

**To toast almonds, spread in single layer on baking sheet. Bake in preheated 350°F oven 8 to 10 minutes or until brown, stirring twice.*

1. Preheat oven to 375°F.

2. Beat powdered sugar and butter in large bowl with electric mixer at medium speed until light and fluffy. Beat in orange peel and liqueur.

3. Set aside 24 whole almonds. Place remaining cooled almonds in food processor. Process using on/off pulsing action until almonds are ground, but not pasty.

4. Place ground almonds, flour and salt in medium bowl; stir to combine. Gradually add to butter mixture. Beat with electric mixer at low speed until well blended.

5. Place dough on lightly floured surface. Roll out dough with lightly floured rolling pin to just under ¼-inch thickness. Cut dough with floured 2½-inch fluted or round cookie cutter. Place dough 2 inches apart on ungreased cookie sheets.

6. Lightly brush tops of cookies with beaten egg. Press one whole reserved almond in center of each cookie. Brush almond lightly with beaten egg. Bake 10 to 12 minutes or until light golden brown.

7. Let cookies stand 1 minute on cookie sheets. Remove cookies with spatula to wire racks; cool completely. Store tightly covered at room temperature, or freeze up to 3 months.

Makes about 2 dozen cookies

Chocolate Cherry Cookies

1 package (8 ounces) sugar-free low-fat chocolate cake mix
3 tablespoons fat-free (skim) milk
½ teaspoon almond extract
10 maraschino cherries, rinsed, drained and cut into halves
2 tablespoons white chocolate chips
½ teaspoon vegetable oil

Preheat oven to 350°F. Spray baking sheets with nonstick cooking spray; set aside.

Beat cake mix, milk and almond extract in medium bowl with electric mixer at low speed. Increase speed to medium when mixture looks crumbly; beat 2 minutes or until smooth dough forms. (Dough will be very sticky.)

Coat hands with cooking spray. Shape dough into 1-inch balls. Place balls 2½ inches apart on prepared baking sheets. Flatten each ball slightly. Place cherry half in center of each cookie.

Bake 8 to 9 minutes or until cookies lose their shininess and tops begin to crack. Do not overbake. Remove to wire racks; cool completely.

Heat white chocolate chips and oil in small saucepan over very low heat until chips melt. Drizzle cookies with melted chips. Allow drizzle to set before serving.

Makes 20 cookies

Norwegian Wreaths

1 hard-cooked egg yolk
1 egg, separated
½ cup butter, softened
½ cup powdered sugar
½ teaspoon vanilla
1¼ cups all-purpose flour
Coarse sugar crystals or crushed sugar cubes

1. Preheat oven to 350°F. Grease cookie sheets; set aside.

2. Beat cooked and raw egg yolks in medium bowl until smooth. Beat in butter, powdered sugar and vanilla. Stir in 1 cup flour. Stir in additional flour until stiff dough forms.

3. Place dough on sheet of waxed paper. Using waxed paper to hold dough, roll it back and forth to form a log; cut into 18 equal pieces. Roll each piece of dough into 8-inch rope, tapering ends.

4. Shape ropes into wreaths; overlap ends and let extend out from wreath. Place wreaths on prepared cookie sheets. Refrigerate 15 minutes or until firm.

5. Beat reserved egg white with fork until foamy. Brush wreaths with egg white; sprinkle with sugar crystals. Bake 8 to 10 minutes or until light golden brown. Remove cookies to wire racks; cool completely.

Makes about 1½ dozen cookies

Viennese Hazelnut Butter Thins

1 cup hazelnuts
1¼ cups all-purpose flour
¼ teaspoon salt
1¼ cups powdered sugar
1 cup butter, softened
1 egg
1 teaspoon vanilla
1 cup semisweet chocolate chips

1. Preheat oven to 350°F. To remove skins from hazelnuts, spread in single layer on baking sheet. Bake 10 to 12 minutes or until toasted and skins begin to flake off; let cool slightly. Wrap hazelnuts in heavy kitchen towel; rub against towel to remove as much of the skins as possible.

2. Place hazelnuts in food processor. Process using on/off pulsing action until hazelnuts are ground but not pasty.

3. Combine flour and salt in small bowl. Beat powdered sugar and butter in medium bowl with electric mixer at medium speed until light and fluffy. Beat in egg and vanilla. Gradually add flour mixture. Beat in ground hazelnuts at low speed until well blended.

4. Place dough on sheet of waxed paper. Using waxed paper to hold dough, roll back and forth to form log 12 inches long and 2½ inches wide. Wrap log in plastic wrap; refrigerate until firm, at least 2 hours or up to 48 hours.

5. Preheat oven to 350°F. Cut dough into ¼-inch-thick slices; place on ungreased cookie sheets.

6. Bake 10 to 12 minutes or until edges are very lightly browned. Let cookies stand on cookie sheets 1 minute. Remove cookies to wire racks; cool completely.

7. Place chocolate chips in 2-cup glass measure. Microwave at HIGH 1 to 1½ minutes or until melted, stirring after 1 minute and at 30-second intervals after first minute.

8. Dip cookies into chocolate, coating about ½ of each cookie, let excess drip back into cup or, spread chocolate on cookies with a narrow spatula. Transfer cookies to waxed paper; let stand at room temperature 1 hour or until set.

Makes about 3 dozen cookies

Note: To store cookies, place in airtight container between layers of waxed paper. Cookies can be frozen for up to 3 months.

Gingerbread People

2¼ cups all-purpose flour
2 teaspoons ground cinnamon
2 teaspoons ground ginger
1 teaspoon baking powder
½ teaspoon salt
¼ teaspoon ground cloves
¼ teaspoon ground nutmeg
¾ cup butter, softened
½ cup packed light brown sugar
½ cup dark molasses
1 egg
Icing (recipe follows) or prepared creamy or gel-type tube frosting (optional)
Candies and other decorations (optional)

1. Combine flour, cinnamon, ginger, baking powder, salt, cloves and nutmeg in large bowl.

2. Beat butter and brown sugar in large bowl until light and fluffy. Beat in molasses and egg. Gradually add flour mixture; beat until well blended. Shape dough into 3 discs. Wrap well in plastic wrap; refrigerate 1 hour or until firm.

3. Preheat oven to 350°F. Working with 1 disc at a time, place on lightly floured surface. Roll out dough with lightly floured rolling pin to 3/16-inch thickness. Cut out gingerbread people with floured 5-inch cookie cutters; place on ungreased cookie sheets. Press dough trimmings together gently; reroll and cut out more cookies.

4. Bake about 12 minutes or until edges are golden brown. Let cookies stand on cookie sheets 1 minute; remove to wire racks to cool completely.

5. Prepare Icing and pipe onto cooled cookies, if desired. Decorate with candies, if desired. Let stand at room temperature 20 minutes or until set. Store tightly covered at room temperature or freeze up to 3 months. *Makes about 16 large cookies*

Icing

2 cups powdered sugar
2 tablespoons milk or lemon juice
Food coloring (optional)

Place powdered sugar and milk in small bowl; stir with spoon until smooth. (Icing will be very thick. If it is too thick, stir in 1 teaspoon additional milk.) Divide into small bowls and tint with food coloring, if desired.

Dear Santa,
Enjoy your
Cookies
and
MiLK!!
Love,
Sara

Mincemeat Pastries

3½ cups all-purpose flour
¾ cup granulated sugar
½ teaspoon salt
½ cup (1 stick) butter, chilled
8 tablespoons vegetable shortening
1 cup buttermilk
1 cup mincemeat
¼ cup powdered sugar (optional)

1. Combine flour, granulated sugar and salt in large bowl; set aside.

2. Cut butter into 1-inch chunks. Add butter and shortening to flour mixture. Cut in with pastry blender or 2 knives until mixture resembles coarse crumbs. Drizzle buttermilk over top; toss just until mixture comes together to form ball.

3. Turn out dough onto lightly floured work surface; fold in half and flatten to about ½ inch thick. Knead about eight times. Divide dough in half; press each half into ½-inch-thick disc. Wrap in plastic wrap and refrigerate at least 30 minutes.

4. Preheat oven to 350°F. Lightly grease cookie sheets; set aside. Let dough rest at room temperature 10 minutes. Roll 1 dough disc into 18×12-inch rectangle on lightly floured work surface. Cut into 24 (3-inch) squares. Place heaping ½ teaspoon mincemeat in center of each square. Fold opposite corners each about ⅔ of the way over filling, overlapping dough corners.

5. Place 2 inches apart on prepared cookie sheets. Repeat with remaining dough.

6. Bake 20 minutes or until lightly browned. Remove cookies to wire racks; cool completely. Sprinkle pastries lightly with powdered sugar, if desired.

Makes 4 dozen cookies

Lemony Cheesecake Bars

1½ cups graham cracker crumbs
⅓ cup sugar
⅓ cup finely chopped pecans
⅓ cup butter or margarine, melted
2 (8-ounce) packages cream cheese, softened
1 (14-ounce) can EAGLE® BRAND Sweetened Condensed Milk (NOT evaporated milk)
2 eggs
½ cup lemon juice from concentrate

1. Preheat oven to 325°F. In medium mixing bowl, combine crumbs, sugar, pecans and melted butter. Reserve ⅓ cup crumb mixture; press remaining mixture firmly on bottom of ungreased 13×9-inch baking pan. Bake 5 minutes. Remove from oven and cool on wire rack.

2. In large mixing bowl, beat cream cheese until fluffy. Gradually beat in Eagle Brand until smooth. Add eggs; beat until just combined. Stir in lemon juice. Carefully spoon mixture onto crust in pan. Spoon reserved crumb mixture to make diagonal stripes on top of cheese mixture or sprinkle to cover.

3. Bake about 30 minutes or until knife inserted near center comes out clean. Cool on wire rack 1 hour. Cut into bars to serve. Store covered in refrigerator.

Makes 3 dozen bars

Prep Time: 25 minutes
Bake Time: 35 minutes

Lemony Cheesecake Bars

Harvest Pumpkin Cookies

2 cups all-purpose flour
1 teaspoon baking powder
1 teaspoon ground cinnamon
½ teaspoon baking soda
½ teaspoon salt
½ teaspoon ground allspice
1 cup butter, softened
1 cup sugar
1 cup canned pumpkin
1 egg
1 teaspoon vanilla
1 cup chopped pecans
1 cup dried cranberries (optional)
Pecan halves (about 36)

Preheat oven to 375°F. Combine flour, baking powder, cinnamon, baking soda, salt and allspice in medium bowl.

Beat butter and sugar in large bowl with electric mixer at medium speed until light and fluffy. Beat in pumpkin, egg and vanilla. Gradually add flour mixture. Beat at low speed until well blended. Stir in chopped pecans and cranberries, if desired.

Drop heaping tablespoonfuls of dough 2 inches apart onto ungreased cookie sheets. Flatten slightly with back of spoon. Press one pecan half into center of each cookie.

Bake 10 to 12 minutes or until golden brown. Let cookies stand on cookie sheets 1 minute; transfer to wire racks to cool completely. Store tightly covered at room temperature or freeze up to 3 months. *Makes about 3 dozen cookies*

Holiday Red Raspberry Chocolate Bars

2½ cups all-purpose flour
1 cup sugar
¾ cup finely chopped pecans
1 cup (2 sticks) cold butter or margarine
1 egg, beaten
1 jar (12 ounces) seedless red raspberry jam
1⅔ cups HERSHEY®S Milk Chocolate Chips, HERSHEY®S Semi-Sweet Chocolate Chips, HERSHEY®S Raspberry Chips, or HERSHEY®S MINI KISSES™ Milk Chocolates

1. Heat oven to 350°F. Grease 13×9×2-inch baking pan.

2. Stir together flour, sugar, pecans, butter and egg in large bowl. Cut in butter with pastry blender or fork until mixture resembles coarse crumbs; set aside 1½ cups crumb mixture. Press remaining crumb mixture on bottom of prepared pan; spread jam over top. Sprinkle with chocolate chips. Crumble remaining crumb mixture evenly over top.

3. Bake 40 to 45 minutes or until lightly browned. Cool completely in pan on wire rack; cut into bars.

Makes 36 bars

Chocolate Sugar Spritz

2 squares (1 ounce each) unsweetened chocolate, coarsely chopped
2¼ cups all-purpose flour
¼ teaspoon salt
1 cup butter, softened
¾ cup granulated sugar
1 large egg
1 teaspoon almond extract
½ cup powdered sugar
1 teaspoon ground cinnamon

1. Preheat oven to 400°F.

2. Melt chocolate in small, heavy saucepan over low heat, stirring constantly. Combine flour and salt in small bowl; stir to combine.

3. Beat butter and granulated sugar in large bowl with electric mixer at medium speed until light and fluffy. Beat in egg and almond extract. Beat in chocolate. Gradually add flour mixture with mixing spoon. (Dough will be stiff.)

4. Fit cookie press with desired plate (or change plates for different shapes after first batch). Fill press with dough; press dough 1 inch apart on ungreased cookie sheets.

5. Bake 7 minutes or until just set. Combine powdered sugar and cinnamon in small bowl. Transfer to fine-mesh strainer and sprinkle over hot cookies while they are still on cookie sheets. Remove cookies to wire racks; cool completely.

6. Store tightly covered at room temperature. These cookies do not freeze well.

Makes 4 to 5 dozen cookies

Rum Fruitcake Cookies

1 cup sugar
¾ cup shortening
3 eggs
⅓ cup orange juice
1 tablespoon rum extract
3 cups all-purpose flour
2 teaspoons baking powder
1 teaspoon baking soda
1 teaspoon salt
2 cups (8 ounces) chopped candied mixed fruit
1 cup raisins
1 cup nuts, coarsely chopped

1. Preheat oven to 375°F. Lightly grease cookie sheets; set aside. Beat sugar and shortening in large bowl until fluffy. Add eggs, orange juice and rum extract; beat 2 minutes.

2. Combine flour, baking powder, baking soda and salt in small bowl. Add candied fruit, raisins and nuts. Stir into creamed mixture. Drop dough by rounded teaspoonfuls 2 inches apart onto prepared cookie sheets. Bake 10 to 12 minutes or until golden. Let cookies stand on cookie sheets 2 minutes. Remove to wire racks; cool completely.

Makes about 6 dozen cookies

Gift-Giving Candies

Cherry Walnut White Chocolate Fudge

3 cups sugar
1 cup whipping cream
½ cup butter
¼ cup light corn syrup
8 ounces premium white chocolate, chopped
1 teaspoon vanilla
1 cup chopped dried cherries
1 cup toasted walnuts, chopped

Spray 9×9-inch pan with nonstick cooking spray. Spray inside of heavy large saucepan.

Combine sugar, cream, butter and syrup in prepared saucepan. Cook over medium heat until sugar dissolves and mixture comes to a boil, stirring frequently. Wash down sugar crystals.

Attach candy thermometer to side of pan, making sure bulb is submerged in sugar mixture but not touching bottom of pan.

Continue cooking about 6 minutes or until sugar mixture reaches soft-ball stage (234°F) on candy thermometer, stirring frequently.

Remove from heat; let stand 10 minutes. (Do not stir.)

Add white chocolate and vanilla; stir 1 minute or until chocolate is melted and mixture is smooth. Stir in cherries and walnuts.

Spread evenly in prepared pan. Score into 64 squares while fudge is still warm.

Refrigerate until firm. Cut along score lines into squares. *Makes 64 candies*

Classic Coconut Bonbons

2 packages (1 pound each) powdered sugar (about 8 cups), divided
1 can (14 ounces) sweetened condensed milk
½ cup butter
2 teaspoons vanilla
2 cups flaked coconut
1 cup finely chopped pecans or walnuts
2 pounds premium bittersweet chocolate

1. Sift ½ of powdered sugar into large bowl with fine-meshed sieve or sifter; set aside.

2. Place sweetened condensed milk and butter in small saucepan; cook over low heat until butter melts and mixture is blended, stirring frequently. Remove from heat; stir in vanilla.

3. Pour hot butter mixture over reserved sifted powdered sugar; beat with electric mixer at medium speed until blended. Sift remaining powdered sugar into bowl; continue to beat until blended and creamy. Stir in coconut and pecans with wooden spoon until combined. Cover with plastic wrap; refrigerate 1 hour.

4. Shape coconut mixture into 1-inch balls. Place on baking sheet lined with waxed paper. Refrigerate until firm.

5. Temper chocolate.

6. Dip balls in tempered chocolate with dipping fork or spoon, tapping handle against side of pan to allow excess chocolate to drain back into pan.

7. Remove excess chocolate by scraping bottom of bonbon across rim of saucepan.

8. Place bonbons on waxed paper. Let stand in cool place until chocolate is firm. (Do not refrigerate.) Store in airtight container at room temperature.

Makes about 10 dozen bonbons (4½ pounds)

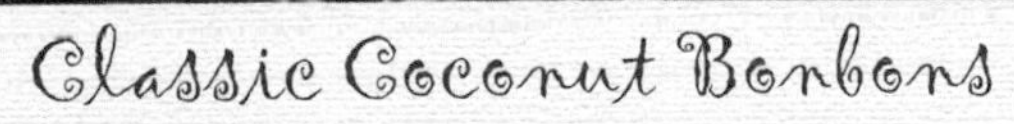
Classic Coconut Bonbons

Elegant Holiday Holly Mints

1 package (3 ounces) cream cheese, softened
3 tablespoons butter or margarine, softened
3 teaspoons liquid green food coloring
½ teaspoon vanilla
¼ teaspoon peppermint extract
1 pound powdered sugar (3½ to 4 cups)
½ cup granulated sugar
1 jar (2 ounces) cinnamon candies

1. Line large cookie sheet with waxed paper; set aside.

2. Beat cream cheese, butter, food coloring, vanilla and peppermint extract in large bowl with electric mixer at medium speed until smooth. Gradually beat in powdered sugar on low speed until well combined, scraping side of bowl several times. (If necessary, stir in remaining powdered sugar with wooden spoon.) Turn out cream cheese mixture onto sheet of waxed paper lightly sprinkled with powdered sugar. Knead dough until smooth and pliable. Place granulated sugar in shallow bowl; set aside.

3. Shape dough into 8½×2¼-inch block. Cut ½-inch slice with long, thin-bladed knife. Place slice on another sheet of waxed paper; flatten gently with fingertips to 3½-inch oval about ¼ inch thick.

4. Transfer slice to bowl with granulated sugar; flip to coat both sides. Return slice to waxed paper; cut two 1½-inch leaves out of slice or use miniature 1½-inch cookie cutter. (If dough becomes too soft to work with, wrap in plastic wrap and refrigerate 15 minutes.) Score veins in leaves. Press cinnamon candies firmly into leaves to resemble berries. Repeat steps with remaining dough and scraps. Place on prepared cookie sheets; refrigerate until firm. Store in airtight container in refrigerator.

Makes about 60 (1½-inch) mints

Elegant Holiday Holly Mints

Peppermint Taffy

2 tablespoons butter, softened and divided
½ cup powdered sugar
2½ cups granulated sugar
½ cup water
¼ cup distilled white vinegar
7 to 8 drops red food coloring
½ teaspoon peppermint extract

1. Butter 12-inch ceramic oval platter or dish with 1 tablespoon butter. Line large baking sheet with foil; sprinkle evenly with powdered sugar.

2. Combine granulated sugar, water, vinegar and remaining 1 tablespoon butter in heavy 2- or 2½-quart saucepan. Bring to a boil, stirring frequently. Attach candy thermometer to side of pan, making sure bulb is submerged in sugar mixture but not touching bottom of pan. Continue boiling, without stirring, about 10 minutes or until sugar mixture reaches between hard-ball stage (265°F) and soft-crack stage (270°F) on candy thermometer. Remove from heat; stir in food coloring and peppermint extract.

3. Slowly pour hot sugar mixture onto prepared platter. Let stand 20 to 25 minutes or until cool enough to handle and an indent made with your finger holds its shape.

4. Remove all jewelry as candy will stick to it. With liberally buttered hands, carefully pick up taffy and shape into a ball. (Center of candy may still be very warm but will cool quickly upon handling). Scrape up any taffy that sticks to plate with rubber spatula.

5. Begin to pull taffy between your hands into a thick rope about 18 inches long while turning and twisting taffy back on itself. Continue pulling taffy about 10 to 15 minutes or until it lightens in color, has a satiny finish and is stiff. (It is important to be patient and pull taffy long enough or the taffy will be sticky.)

6. When taffy begins to hold the folds of the rope shape and develops ridges in the rope, begin pulling 1-inch-wide ropes from taffy and let ropes fall onto prepared powdered sugar surface. Cut each rope with buttered kitchen shears. Cut taffy ropes into 1-inch pieces using shears. Cool completely; wrap individually in waxed paper. Store in airtight container at room temperature up to 1 week.

Makes about 1 pound taffy

Lemon Taffy: Substitute 4 to 5 drops yellow food coloring for the red, and lemon extract for the peppermint. Proceed as directed above.

Butter Toffee Crunch

¾ cup butter or margarine
1 tablespoon corn syrup
Hot water
1 cup sugar
1 package (2¼ ounces) sliced almonds (about ¾ cup)

1. Place butter in 2-quart microwave-safe bowl. Microwave at HIGH 1 minute or until melted.

2. Stir in corn syrup, 2 tablespoons hot water and sugar. Microwave at HIGH 4 minutes, stirring after 1 minute. Add 1 tablespoon hot water; stir to combine. Microwave at HIGH 1 minute.

3. Stir in almonds. Microwave at HIGH 2 to 3 minutes, until light caramel in color.

4. Pour onto an ungreased baking sheet. Spread out candy. Cool until set. Break into pieces. Store in airtight container.

Makes about ¾ pound

Variation: Sprinkle hot candy with 1 cup milk chocolate chips. Let melt; spread.

Hint: If kitchen is cold, warm baking sheet before pouring out toffee. It will spread more easily and be thinner.

Glazed Almonds

1 cup blanched whole almonds (about 5 ounces)
⅓ cup water
1 tablespoon corn syrup
1 cup sugar

1. Spread almonds in microwave-safe pie pan. Microwave at HIGH 3 minutes, stirring after every minute. Almonds should be lightly toasted.

2. Butter baking sheet; set aside. Lightly butter side of microwave-safe 2-quart dish.

3. Combine water, corn syrup and sugar in prepared 2-quart dish. Microwave at HIGH 2 minutes; stir. Microwave on HIGH 5 minutes.

4. Using dipping fork or table fork, dip one almond at a time in syrup. Remove excess syrup by scraping bottom of almonds across rim of dish. Place almonds on prepared baking sheet. (If syrup begins to harden, microwave at HIGH 1 minute; stir.) Cool at room temperature until set.

5. Store loosely covered at room temperature.

Makes about 1 cup

Top to bottom: Butter Toffee Crunch and Glazed Almonds

Merri-Mint Truffles

1 package (10 ounces) mint chocolate chips
⅓ cup whipping cream
¼ cup butter or margarine
1 container (3½ ounces) chocolate sprinkles

Melt chocolate chips with cream and butter in heavy medium saucepan over low heat, stirring occasionally. Pour into pie pan. Refrigerate about 2 hours or until mixture is fudgy, but soft.

Shape about 1 tablespoonful of mixture into 1¼-inch ball. Repeat with remaining mixture. Roll balls in your palms to form uniform round shapes; place on waxed paper.

Place sprinkles in shallow bowl. Roll balls in sprinkles; place in petit four or candy cases. (If coating mixture won't stick because truffle has set, roll between your palms until outside is soft.) Store in airtight container up to 3 days in refrigerator or several weeks in freezer.

Makes about 24 truffles

Easy Orange Truffles

1 cup (6 ounces) semisweet chocolate chips
2 squares (1 ounce each) unsweetened chocolate, chopped
1½ cups powdered sugar
½ cup butter or margarine, softened
1 tablespoon grated orange peel
1 tablespoon orange-flavored liqueur
2 squares (1 ounce each) semisweet chocolate, grated or cocoa powder

Melt chocolate chips and unsweetened chocolate in heavy small saucepan over very low heat, stirring constantly; set aside.

Combine powdered sugar, butter, orange peel and liqueur in small bowl. Beat with electric mixer until combined. Beat in cooled chocolate. Pour into pie pan. Refrigerate about 30 minutes or until mixture is fudgy and can be shaped into balls.

Shape scant 1 tablespoonful of mixture into 1-inch ball. Repeat with remaining mixture. Roll balls in your palms to form uniform round shapes; place on waxed paper.

Sprinkle grated chocolate in shallow bowl. Roll balls in grated chocolate; place in petit four or candy cases. (If coating mixture won't stick because truffle has set, roll between your palms until outside is soft.) Store in airtight container up to 3 days in refrigerator or several weeks in freezer.

Makes about 34 truffles

Left to right: Merri-Mint Truffles, Easy Orange Truffles and Jolly Bourbon Balls

Jolly Bourbon Balls

1 package (12 ounces) vanilla wafers, finely crushed (3 cups)
1 cup finely chopped nuts
1 cup powdered sugar, divided
1 cup (6 ounces) semisweet chocolate chips
½ cup light corn syrup
⅓ cup bourbon or rum

Combine crushed wafers, nuts and ½ cup powdered sugar in large bowl; set aside.

Melt chocolate with corn syrup in top of double boiler over simmering (not boiling) water. Stir in bourbon until smooth. Pour chocolate mixture over crumb mixture; stir to combine thoroughly. Shape scant 1 tablespoonful of mixture into 1-inch ball. Repeat with remaining mixture. Roll balls in your palms to form uniform round shapes; place on waxed paper.

Place remaining ½ cup powdered sugar in shallow bowl. Roll balls in powdered sugar; place in petit four or candy cases. Store in airtight containers at least 3 days before serving for flavors to mellow. (May be stored up to 2 weeks.)

Makes about 48 candies

Candy Cane Fudge

- ½ cup whipping cream
- ½ cup light corn syrup
- 3 cups semisweet chocolate chips
- 1½ cups powdered sugar, sifted
- 1 cup candy canes, crushed
- 1½ teaspoons vanilla extract

Line 8-inch baking pan with foil, extending edges over sides of pan.

Bring cream and corn syrup to a boil in 2-quart saucepan over medium heat. Boil 1 minute. Remove from heat. Stir in chocolate. Cook until chocolate is melted, stirring constantly. Stir in powdered sugar, candy canes and vanilla. Pour into prepared pan. Spread mixture into corners. Cover; refrigerate 2 hours or until firm.

Lift fudge out of pan using foil; remove foil. Cut into 1-inch squares. Store in airtight container.

Makes about 2 pounds or 64 pieces

Almond Butter Crunch

- 1 cup BLUE DIAMOND® Blanched Slivered Almonds
- ½ cup butter
- ½ cup sugar
- 1 tablespoon light corn syrup

Line bottom and sides of 8- or 9-inch cake pan with aluminum foil (not plastic wrap or wax paper). Butter foil heavily; set aside. Combine almonds, butter, sugar and corn syrup in 10-inch skillet. Bring to a boil over medium heat, stirring constantly. Boil, stirring constantly, until mixture turns golden brown, about 5 to 6 minutes. Working quickly, spread candy in prepared pan. Cool about 15 minutes or until firm. Remove candy from pan by lifting edges of foil. Peel off foil. Cool thoroughly. Break into pieces.

Makes about ¾ pound

Candy Cane Fudge

Decadent Truffle Tree

Ingredients

1⅓ cups whipping cream
¼ cup packed brown sugar
¼ teaspoon salt
¼ cup light rum
2 teaspoons vanilla
16 ounces semisweet chocolate, chopped
16 ounces milk chocolate, chopped
Finely chopped nuts and assorted sprinkles

Supplies

1 (9-inch tall) foam cone
About 70 wooden toothpicks

1. Heat cream, sugar, salt, rum and vanilla in medium saucepan over medium heat until sugar is dissolved and mixture is hot. Remove from heat; add chocolates, stirring until melted, (return pan to low heat if necessary). Pour into shallow dish. Cover and refrigerate until just firm, about 1 hour.

2. Shape about half the mixture into 1¼-inch balls. Shape remaining mixture into ¾-inch balls. Roll balls in nuts and sprinkles. Refrigerate truffles until firm, about 1 hour.

3. Cover cone with foil. Starting at bottom of cone, attach larger truffles with wooden toothpicks. Use smaller truffles toward the top of the cone. Refrigerate until serving time.

Makes 1 tree (6 dozen truffles)

Note: If kitchen is very warm, keep portion of truffle mixture chilled as you shape and roll balls.

Black and White Caramels

Caramels

- **2 cups sugar**
- **2 cups light corn syrup**
- **1 cup half-and-half**
- **1 cup unsalted butter**
- **½ teaspoon salt**
- **1 cup whipping cream**
- **1 teaspoon vanilla**

Coating

- **12 ounces semisweet chocolate, chopped**
- **14 to 16 ounces white chocolate, chopped and divided**
- **6 teaspoons shortening**

1. To prepare caramels, line 8-inch square pan with heavy-duty foil, pressing foil into corners to cover completely and leaving 1-inch overhang on sides. Lightly butter foil.

2. Combine sugar, corn syrup, half-and-half, butter and salt in heavy 4½-quart saucepan. Bring to a boil over medium-high heat, stirring occasionally. Wash down sugar crystals with pastry brush, if necessary. Continue boiling 25 minutes or until sugar mixture reaches firm-ball stage (244° to 246°F) on candy thermometer, stirring frequently. Remove from heat; very gradually stir in cream.

3. Return to medium heat. Cook 15 minutes or until mixture reaches 248°F on candy thermometer, stirring frequently. Remove from heat; stir in vanilla. Immediately pour into prepared pan. (Do not scrape saucepan.) Cool at room temperature 3 to 4 hours or until firm.

4. Remove caramels from pan, lifting by foil handles. Place on cutting board; peel off foil. Cut into 1-inch strips with long, thin-bladed knife. Cut each strip into 1-inch squares with buttered knife or kitchen shears. Line two 13×9-inch baking pans with waxed paper; lightly butter paper. Place squares ¾ inch apart in prepared pans. Cover tightly with plastic wrap and let stand overnight at room temperature.

5. To prepare coating, temper or melt semisweet chocolate. Lower caramels into tempered chocolate with dipping fork or spoon (do not pierce), tapping handle gently against side of pan to allow excess chocolate to drain back into pan. Remove excess chocolate by scraping bottom of caramel across rim of saucepan.

6. Place caramels on waxed paper. Let stand in cool place until chocolate is firm. (Do not refrigerate.)

7. Place 12 ounces white chocolate and all of shortening in clean double boiler; temper or melt. Dip remaining caramels as directed in Step 5. As soon as white chocolate starts to thicken too much, return top pan to double boiler momentarily; stir in 1 additional ounce white chocolate until mixture loosens. Continue dipping, adding remaining white chocolate as needed, until all caramels are coated.

8. Store coated caramels in airtight container at room temperature.

Makes 64 (1-inch) caramels

Rich Chocolate Pumpkin Truffles

2½ cups (about 62) crushed vanilla wafers
1 cup ground almonds, toasted
¾ cup sifted powdered sugar, *divided*
2 teaspoons ground cinnamon
1 cup (6 ounces) NESTLÉ® TOLL HOUSE® Semi-Sweet Chocolate Morsels, melted*
½ cup LIBBY'S® 100% Pure Pumpkin
⅓ cup coffee liqueur or apple juice

**Follow melting direction on NESTLÉ® package.*

COMBINE crushed cookies, ground almonds, *½ cup* powdered sugar and cinnamon in medium bowl. Blend in melted chocolate, pumpkin and coffee liqueur. Shape into 1-inch balls. Refrigerate. Dust with *remaining* powdered sugar just before serving.

Makes 4 dozen candies

Fruit Bars

1 cup chopped figs
1 cup chopped dates
1 cup chopped dried pears
1 cup finely chopped pecans
¼ cup orange marmalade

1. Butter 8-inch square pan; set aside.
2. Combine all ingredients in medium bowl. Press mixture in prepared pan. Refrigerate until set.
3. Cut into bars. Store in refrigerator.

Makes 32 bars

The publisher would like to thank the companies and organizations listed below for the use of their recipes and photographs in this publication.

Birds Eye®
Blue Diamond Growers®
Bob Evans®
Butterball® Turkey
California Wild Rice Advisory Board
Cherry Marketing Institute
Dole Food Company, Inc.
Duncan Hines® and Moist Deluxe® are registered trademarks of Aurora Foods Inc.
Eagle Brand®
Fleischmann's® Yeast
Grandma's® is a registered trademark of Mott's, Inc.
Heinz North America
Hershey Foods Corporation
The Hidden Valley® Food Products Company
Holland House® is a registered trademark of Mott's, Inc.
Keebler® Company
Lawry's® Foods
McIlhenny Company (TABASCO® brand Pepper Sauce)
Minnesota Cultivated Wild Rice Council
Mott's® is a registered trademark of Mott's, Inc.
National Honey Board
National Pork Board
National Turkey Federation
Nestlé USA
Reckitt Benckiser Inc.
StarKist® Seafood Company
The Sugar Association, Inc.
TexaSweet Citrus Marketing, Inc.
Uncle Ben's Inc.
Unilever Bestfoods North America
USA Rice Federation
Walnut Marketing Board
Washington Apple Commission

Index